"[A] charming memoir . . . [with] magical moments."

—*The New York Times Book Review*

"*Hit by a Farm* is heartening, sweet, earthy, funny—a joy to read from start to finish."

—*Minneapolis Star-Tribune*

"*Hit by a Farm* is a thoroughly engaging romp for all. This is a must-read for any city girl who's ever whiled away an hour or two dreaming about the bucolic existence of her rural sisters."

—*Bust*

"[I]rresistable. . . . *Hit by a Farm* goes beyond funny, through poignant, sad, and angry, to redemptive: all the things that make a farm—and a relationship—successful."

—*Lavender*

"This honest look at collaboration and compromise, the pain and the joy of partnership, and the hands-on of farming will find a ready audience."

—*Booklist*

"[A] multi-mood, clever and unpredictable tale of what makes farm life far from mundane and sheltered . . . *Hit by a Farm* slyly educates as it entertains, heals as it humors us while wading through issues of confrontation, complications, and compromise . . . a treasure."

—*Madison Capital Times*

"Tractor mommas, this is the book for you!"

—Rita Mae Brown

"*Hit by a Farm* is not the kind of book I'd normally pick up. While farming is central to my culinary life, the romance of living on the land hardly appeals to someone who, when forced to weed a small flower garden, screams loudly that she is NOT a pioneer!

That's why I was so surprised that I simply could not put the book down. Catherine Friend is a luscious writer. She packs this memoir of two women starting a farm together in Southern Minnesota with hilarity, tenderness, grim reality and suspense. This memoir is, hands down, the best story I've read in ages."

—ELLEN HART, author of 21 mystery novels,
five-time winner of the Lambda Literary Award

"What a funny, touching delightful, *human* story! Catherine is not only a farmer; she is most certainly a writer too."

—MARION DANE BAUER, Newbery Honor Book author

"*Hit by a Farm* is both heartbreaking and hilarious. Catherine Friend's clear and vivid writing in this fine, funny, unflinching book put me right on the farm, manure and all, through disasters and triumphs. Friend has taken the stuff of her life and made literature out of it."

—PHYLLIS ROOT, faculty of Vermont College MFA program

"If you ever thought farming could be a fabulous back-to-basics adventure, if you ever wondered about the difference in raising, say, a sheep or a peacock, if you ever wanted an honest—but jaundiced—peek at farm living, read Catherine Friend's *Hit by a Farm*. You'll be hit by her candor and humor, and your thoughts about farming will never be the same."

—CINDY ROGERS, author, *Word Magic for Writers*, childhood farmer

catherine friend farms in Minnesota with her partner of twenty-two years. The author of five children's books, with a sixth forthcoming in 2007, Catherine would rather write than wrangle sheep, but is proud she can do both. She works as a freelance editor, volunteers in her community, and wishes Elvis were still alive. Visit her at www.hitbyafarm.com

hit by a farm

hit by a farm

*How I Learned to Stop Worrying
and Love the Barn*

catherine friend

marlowe & company
new york

Hit by a Farm:
How I Learned to Stop Worrying and Love the Barn
Copyright © 2006 by Catherine Friend

Published by
Marlowe & Company
An Imprint of Avalon Publishing Group, Incorporated
245 West 17th Street • 11th Floor
New York, NY 10011-5300

AVALON

Library of Congress Cataloging-in-Publication Data
Friend, Catherine.
Hit by a farm : how I learned to stop worrying and love the barn /
Catherine Friend.
p. cm.
ISBN 1-56924-298-4
1. Farm life—Minnesota. 2. Friend, Catherine. I. Title.
S521.5.M6F75 2006
630.9776—dc22   2005037255

ISBN-13: 978-1-56924-298-8

9 8 7 6 5 4

Designed by Pauline Neuwirth, Neuwirth & Associates, Inc.

Printed in the United States of America

To my late grandparents,
Albert and Florence Friend
Elmer and Nora LaRiviere

contents

PART I **romancing the farm** 1

Touching Testicles 3

Hooked on Romance 7

Goodbye, City Life 12

Baby on Our Doorstep 18

Wild Hairs 23

Even My Bra *Was More Supportive* 30

A Paper Farm 34

Shepherds at Last 42

Wild Woolies 46

Can't Fit into My Grandma's Genes 51

Chicken Run 54

Ménage à Trois 58

A Grape Disaster 60

Read the Directions, Dummy 64

A Shocking Story 68

To Market, to Market 72

Oops 76

Finding Our Way in the Dark 82

Chicken Sex 86

At Long Last, Sheep Sex 88

PART 2: hit by a farm   95

What Could Possibly Go Wrong?   97
Dancing with Goats in the Moonlight   101
Time to Take It Off (The Wool, That Is)   103
In the Bedroom   108
Ready or Not, Here They Come   111
The First Bad Day   115
Ear Tags and Little Rubber Bands   117
Another Bad Day, but Who's Counting?   120
Searching for Placenta by Moonlight   125
High Anxiety   128
Having Fun Yet?   132
Lying through My Teeth   137
Serge and Sonny   141
Let's Just Forget This Ever Happened   145
Meeting My Meat   148
Sexing Brenda   154
Lambing: The Dreaded Sequel   157
The Goat Queen   161
Drowning in Dreams   164
Coyotes and Paper Plates   168
The Sixteen-inch Llama   173
The Only Good Goose Is a Dead Goose   177
If It's in a Book, It Must Be True   181
Mermaid Dreams   185
Ducks and Tattoos   189
Small Losses   192
Lesbians and Straight Lines   195
Nature's Sentimental Journey   198

PART 3: the tattoo of transformation, sort of . . .   203

More Loss   205
Shadowboxing   213

I Build a Fence   217
Ruby Jumps Over the Fence   223
Back in the Saddle Again   228
Epilogue: Still Crazy After All These Years   234

Acknowledgments   239

PART

1

romancing the farm

touching testicles

farms have fences. People have boundaries. Mine began crumbling the day I knelt behind a male sheep, reached between his legs, and squeezed his testicles. This unsettling event took place the blustery November day when I joined a group of shepherd-wannabes for a weekend class on the basics of raising sheep. I was there with my partner, Melissa, the woman I'd lived with and loved for twelve years, because we were going to start a farm.

Janet, the course instructor, had motioned us closer. "Grab his testicles here, around the widest part," she commanded. I shot a look of panic to Melissa. Janet wanted us to what? We moved in to hear her over the frigid wind. "Ram testicles should be about sixteen inches around," she said.

I huddled closer to Melissa as I tried to stay warm in my leather aviator jacket, red scarf, and white sneakers. My head was numb from the cold, but a hat was out of the question because I would not appear in public with "hat hair." I snuggled down as far as I could into my collar, and realized something soft and lumpy was stuck to the bottom of my sneaker. Melissa wore a heavy winter coat, a massive wool hat with flaps, bulky winter snow boots. She looked ridiculous.

She also looked warm. I pressed my upturned collar to my icy ears as Janet nodded to Melissa and me. We were next.

I stepped forward and stood behind the sturdy ram locked in a head gate, calmly chewing his cud. Sixteen inches. Cripes. Skeptical, I moved closer. "You sure he won't mind?"

"Positive," Janet said. Her long gray hair whirled around her reddened face and she wasn't even wearing gloves. "You need to know what healthy ram testicles feel like. Grasp them firmly, feeling for any soft spots or hard lumps."

Right. No problem. The ram, built like a small chest freezer, had stood still while seven other couples fiddled with him. Melissa danced in place beside me, eager for her turn.

I knelt behind the ram, whose thighs narrowed to tiny sharp hooves that looked dainty but deadly. His cropped tail covered his anus, but small dried hunks of manure clung to the edges of his wool. Please don't poop now, I prayed as I leaned forward.

"C'mon, Cath, you can do it," Melissa said, practically trembling with enthusiasm.

I moaned under my breath. What on *earth* was I thinking? At that very moment most of my friends were attending a writing conference in St. Paul. They were warm, clean, and didn't have anything soft and lumpy stuck to their sneaker bottoms. They were discussing point of view, character development, and the latest publishing information. Their boundaries were intact enough that they were not feeling up a ram with sixteen-inch testicles.

Wincing, I reached between the ram's back legs with my thumb and forefinger.

"Don't *pinch* him," Janet cried.

By now the rest of the class had turned to watch. Embarrassed, I took a deep breath and wrapped both hands around the pendulous testicles. They were warm, squishy, and woolly. I squeezed gently, wondering briefly if this was the ram's favorite part of the course.

I let go and shot to my feet. "Okay, next?"

"Me, me," Melissa whispered as she dropped to her knees and immediately began poking and prodding the poor guy, even craning around his hip to stare at his penis. The books we'd read had said when you buy a ram you should manipulate the penis to collect a semen sample for testing. Even Melissa, a hands-on person if there ever was one, had reservations about this procedure. Luckily Janet hadn't included it in the weekend's curriculum.

I stuffed my hands into my pockets. My eyes watered from the wind. I wanted to be warm. I wanted to be working on my new children's book, which had nothing whatsoever to do with ram testicles. But instead I hunched over against the wind and followed the class to the next task, which involved wrestling a two-hundred-pound ewe from a standing position back onto her rump.

The bored ewe stood there as, one by one, the class members grasped her under the chin, then under her tail. They grunted and groaned and twisted her back, but few were successful. I was too damn frozen to even think about taking my hands out of my pockets. I'd lost all feeling in my face, fingers, and feet. Melissa tackled the leggy ewe with enthusiasm, and was nearly successful, until the fed-up ewe twisted, turned, and darted through Melissa's legs. With a whoop, Melissa suddenly found herself *riding* the ewe, backwards. We laughed so hard I thought my cheeks would crack in the cold.

Melissa and I had laughed our way through crises and misunderstandings and disagreements. We shared a bed, a bank account, and—after Melissa's energetic campaigning years earlier—we shared an underwear drawer, my size 7s commingling twenty-four hours a day with her size 5s. Sharing an underwear drawer had seemed a small and easy concession, but apparently underwear-mingling is a slippery slope, one of life's dangers they never mentioned in Health Class. Underwear-mingling can lead straight to the more disastrous sharing of dreams, because Melissa wanted me to share her dream—of owning a farm, of living on that farm, of *being* a farmer.

Farming had never been my dream. My dream was to grow my writing career into something I could call "successful," whatever that was. I'd already sold two children's books and a handful of magazine stories. I was hungry for more.

Could our dreams of farming and writing coexist? Why not? *Charlotte's Web* creator E. B. White had been a great writer, and he farmed. Ernest Hemingway had used Key West as a romantic place to write. Hadn't the Brontë sisters lived isolated lives? I could imagine myself sitting under the spreading canopy of a mature oak tree, penning a best-selling novel while our wide, green fields glistened in the sun. I'd collected most of my knowledge of country living from art, so I was pretty sure we'd have haystacks like Monet's. We'd lounge around in the shade and drink lemonade like in a Renoir. We'd live the quaint life painted by Grandma Moses.

Unfortunately, I did not realize that once you've squeezed ram testicles, all your well-maintained boundaries collapse and chaos moves in. Would I help Melissa farm? My life with her had led me on many adventures I'd have otherwise missed, so what harm could one more do? The classic face of farming in Grant Wood's *American Gothic* was about to get a facelift: two thirty-something women in bib overalls holding pitchforks.

It turns out that, at age thirty-eight, I knew myself about as well as I knew the breeding habits of the Pygmy Butterfly, which is to say, not at all. So when I answered Melissa's request to help her start the farm with a hearty yes, I might as well have stood on the center line of a four-lane highway and opened my arms. I would witness chicken sex. I would witness duck sex. I would even get frightfully involved in sex between two goats, something no feminist should ever have to face. I would also totally lose myself to my partner's life—gosh, surely the first woman to do so—and would come to question whether my size 7s really *did* belong in the same drawer with Melissa's size 5s.

hooked on romance

boundaries are good things; they're the signposts we use during our lives to measure just how far we'll go. My boundaries have always served me well. No touching worms or spiders or anything gross. No touching wild animals because they could be dangerous. No touching of feces, urine, blood, or any other bodily fluid. Definitely *no* sticking my hand up inside an animal's body, or touching it anywhere I wouldn't want to be touched myself. No taking physical risks.

The safest way to explore the world was between the covers of a book. The boundaries of my childhood were limited only by my ability to bike down the scary Brackett Street hill to the Eau Claire Public Library and check out more books. On those rainy Saturdays when I couldn't get to the library, my boundaries narrowed to four walls and a younger sister pestering me to play Beauty Parlor. I'd braid her hair quickly, then return to my book.

I spent my childhood either with my nose in Trixie Belden or *The Happy Hollisters,* or lost in romantic fantasies. When I was ten, I played for hours with my blue plastic Jane West doll and her plastic palomino. Living in a small university city in Wisconsin with my parents and sister, I dreamt of a blue-eyed, black-haired cowboy on a snow-white stallion who'd sweep me off my feet. I had a hamster, Susie, who died.

When I was twelve, I snuggled down into our basement sofa, surrounded by orange shag carpet so long we raked it rather than vacuumed it, and read Nancy Drew mysteries over and over again, not at all drawn to the outdoor neighborhood games led by my tomboy sister. Inside I wove my own extraordinary life of adventure, a life filled with good chums, a sporty convertible, and a handsome boyfriend tall enough to look me in the eye. I had a cat, Nikki, who died.

At fourteen, I read so constantly that my parents were forced to set a "No reading at the table" rule. Leon Uris and Robert Ludlum and Mary Stewart caught me up in danger and intrigue that thrilled but never threatened. Little Joe from *Bonanza* was just the cowboy I sought, even though he rode a black and white pinto instead of a white stallion. Under the stereo headphones I listened for hours to the Osmond Brothers sing "You've Lost That Lovin' Feeling," and dreamt about Jay, the drummer. *Star Trek* fueled my dreams that Captain Kirk would beam down and beg me to join him forever on the *Enterprise*. I had a beagle named Molly, a dog my parents eventually "moved" to the country because she wouldn't stop using our basement as her toilet. She was torn from my life just as surely as if she had died.

About two hundred miles away, Melissa lived a childhood entirely different from mine. She chased after frogs and toads, picked up smooth garter snakes, caught turtles and skinks, and dissected the dead squirrel she and her two brothers found under the oak tree in the front yard. She teased her twin sister and hated math. She collected bugs, both dead and alive.

She built backyard bunkers and foxholes for playing war with her brothers. She cared for baby raccoons, baby ducks, baby birds, rabbits, goldfish, and a seahorse named Toby. She either nursed sick animals back to health, or gave them respectful burials out back. She picked up and examined sleeping bats, fascinated.

As a teenager, she played moody, love-tormented songs on the guitar, hit archery targets at camp, learned to identify wildflowers and native grasses and how to tell the difference between a spruce and a fir tree. She could build a one-match fire, and dreamed of one day driving big machinery like the county snow-plow that barreled through massive snowdrifts, spraying cold sparkles ten feet into the air.

One day I looked up from *Wuthering Heights* to discover I was an adult. Little Joe hadn't swept me off my feet, and I'd sold Jane West and her horse in a garage sale. Jay Osmond never appeared in my life, and Scotty never beamed Captain Kirk down into my bedroom. I loved animals, but had never had much hands-on success.

Life continued as I kept reading, watching, and dreaming. I had spent my adolescence nursing crushes on Little Joe and Captain Kirk because I was in love with the idea of romance, and society packaged romance in the shape of a strong, attractive man. But in reality I just couldn't connect with men. In college I dated both men and women. I fell in love with one woman, and we were together, on and off, for four years, then I fell in love with another, and we were together for two.

But now it was 1983, and I was once again single, a gay urban professional, or "guppy." I sat in my one-bedroom Twin Cities apartment overlooking a row of garages and the railroad tracks that ran past Como Park, staring at the personal ads in the *City Pages* and talking to myself. What was a hopeless romantic doing reading personal ads? I'd never find what I sought in there. Only losers place those ads! Only losers answer those ads! Why did I expect the written word to solve all my problems? Get a grip, woman. Get dressed and do what every other woman did to meet someone, male or female—go to a bar.

But I hated bars and was allergic to smoke. My college dorm and grad school had worked well in the past as places to meet people. By this point I was an economist for a state agency, but all the women at work were straight, and I'd met all my friends' single friends. I was dangerously close to thirty. Who would want me then? Fast running out of ideas, I would live the rest of my life alone, unloved. Oh, for heaven's sake.

One of the ads seemed less threatening: *Very attractive blonde lesbian, 25, 5'9", 125 lbs. Would like to meet resp. caring 20–30 yr old monogamous woman. Send note and I'll call.* I penned a timid response, blathering on about how friendship was more important than anything, then sent it.

She called and my mouth dried out faster than morning dew on the Mojave. "My hairdresser suggested I answer an ad," I stammered.

"My hairdresser *wrote* mine," she admitted with a hearty laugh.

We agreed to meet at the Como Park Pavilion. "How will I know who you are?" I asked, a strange thrill running up my spine, as if I were an international spy. A secret sign or password? A carnation on her lapel? Would she offer to light my cigarette? Wait. I didn't smoke.

"I have a reddish-brown dog named Sasha. She'll be with me."

Oh.

Because I lived on the other side of the lake, I had to walk around half the lake to reach the Pavilion. As I did I passed a woman walking a reddish-brown dog. She was tall, slender, and lanky, wearing black and white high-tops, jeans, a shirt, and brown suede jacket. Her long, narrow face was softened by the explosion of dark blonde curls billowing around her shoulders. She looked wild, sensual, out of control. No, she looked like a seventeen-year-old boy. No, she looked like a woman who knew herself and what she wanted. No, she became a seventeen-year-old boy again. Androgyny alert. My palms began to sweat. My pulse pounded in my ears. Why had I ever thought this would be a good idea?

I reached the appointed meeting place but no one was there,

so I paced, trying to look cool and casual rather than petrified. Finally the reddish-brown dog I'd seen earlier ran around the corner of the Pavilion and approached me, long slender nose nuzzling my hand. Sasha. Behind her followed the lanky woman with the wild hair. Damn. I swallowed hard. How would I make it through the next hour?

But as we walked and talked, she didn't seem so tough. Melissa may have looked like a seventeen-year-old boy, but she was a woman. We talked about our childhoods, and how she'd raised every critter imaginable. "What did you do?" she asked.

"I read . . . a lot," I confessed, suddenly wishing I had lettered on the high-school tennis team or climbed Mount Everest or done *something*. By the time we reached the halfway mark—Como is not a huge lake—I figured out Melissa was incredibly sensitive and vulnerable, desperately needing a friend in her life who wouldn't hurt her. I could be that friend, I decided, but only a friend. It was too scary to consider anything else, and besides, she was too cute to be interested in me.

We approached a bench. "Want to sit for awhile?" I asked. The Pavilion was coming up quickly, and I was actually enjoying myself too much to return to my empty apartment. The wide wooden bench had shed most of the recent rain, but a few drops still glimmered in the late afternoon sun.

"No, wait. Not yet," she said, then pulled a brown plastic garbage bag from her coat and a massive pocketknife from her jeans pocket. My eyes popped wide open—a woman with a pocketknife. She neatly sliced the bag the long way and laid it out across the bench. "There, that's better," she said, sweeping an open hand toward the bench. The ground opened up, and my heart tumbled in. By the end of that year, my blue-eyed, black-haired cowboy turned into a blonde, green-eyed woman, nearly as tall as I was. She was Little Joe, Jay Osmond, James T. Kirk, *and* Nancy Drew all rolled into one. I was set for life, baby.

goodbye, city life

f **or the next** eleven years, our lives were no more, no less interesting than those of other urban couples as we dealt with job
changes, school, moves, and family crises. At thirty-six, Melissa no
longer sometimes looked like a seventeen-year-old boy. She now
sometimes looked like a nineteen-year-old boy. At thirty-seven,
I looked, well, thirty-seven. Melissa's healthy appetite for ice
cream had encouraged my own, so I'd bumped up a jean size.
Okay, two. As Anne Lamott wrote in one of her novels, "Happiness weighs more." We had been through a lot together, and even
though the state of Minnesota would not issue us a certificate, we
were married in every sense of the word. Every day that we
began and ended together reaffirmed our commitment to each
other. That commitment, our commingled underwear, and laughter, kept us together.

We lived in a townhouse with a small fenced backyard that
stretched only about twenty feet by twenty feet. I didn't appreciate then how little psychic energy it took to own four hundred
square feet, and was later to think back with great nostalgia and
affection for this tiny acreage, small enough I could stand in the
middle with our electric mower and mow the lawn practically

without moving. Like many urbanites, I yearned for more space, more breathing room.

But when Melissa wanted us to leave the city for small town life, I suddenly wasn't sure. I would have to leave my lucrative job as a technical writer, as well as leave behind the potential to earn even more money in the future. And just think—no more theater, which, actually, we rarely attended. No large malls, which we rarely walked. No big-city festivals, which we avoided because Melissa hated crowds.

Could I do this? Weren't small towns full of hicks and rednecks? Wouldn't they harass two lesbians? I hated change. My parents told me they once moved the living-room furniture out of position a few inches to see how long it took me to make things right again. This is probably as close as my parents got to child abuse.

Part of me yearned to shake things up, to try something new, to have another adventure with Melissa. If I left technical writing, maybe I could spend more time pursuing my interest in creative writing. The romance of rural life beckoned. The stress just had to be lower outside the city.

Melissa took a job with the USDA as a soil conservationist, and was transferred to a small southeast Minnesota town of two thousand souls. We bought a tiny gray house, complete with the clichéd white picket fence. The house's parquet floor and silent electric heat charmed me, but I was totally unnerved by the town's inhabitants. As I walked our dogs, total strangers drove by and waved at me. Why? Had they mistaken me for someone else? I eventually started waving back. When I ran errands in the cozy, two-block downtown, total strangers smiled and said hi. Why? What did they want? I eventually started smiling back, and they were no longer strangers. Soon the postmaster and the pharmacist and the dentist's receptionist all called me by name. I loved the entire town and stopped driving sixty miles back to the Twin Cities to shop. If these generous small-town people, none of them appearing to be rednecked hicks, had any problem with two women living together, we didn't hear about it. It turns out there was already another lesbian couple in town, so our arrival barely made a splash.

During the three years we lived in town, I began writing children's books, and joined two writing groups. Thanks to several strokes of good luck, I sold two picture book manuscripts to a major publisher, and they would become real books. I took classes, sold some short stories to a handful of children's magazines, and struggled with the insecurities that came from this audacious pursuit. Determination gripped me, however, as I had never enjoyed anything as much as I enjoyed turning an idea into a story, and every time it happened, I marveled at my satisfaction. It was awkward trying to explain this to nonwriters, so I found myself seeking out writing friends. Melissa read all my stories willingly, and developed her gentle critique skills. I was a writer. It was a heady thing. Life was good.

One summer evening as the setting sun cast our front stoop in shadow, we sat outside reading, our dogs, Tory and Amber, happily chewing on sticks at our feet. Tory was a springer/lab mix whose long ears were covered in curls, and Amber was a German short-haired pointer, sweet but nervous. (We'd had to put Sasha to sleep years ago after she weakened with inoperable liver cancer.)

I read the latest issue of *Writer's Digest*. As a USDA employee, Melissa got on lots of mailing lists, so she sat beside me reading the Murray McMurray poultry catalog—chickens, ducks, geese, exotic birds. "Look at these Silver Spangled Hamburgs! Aren't they amazing? Or these Speckled Sussex. It says these Araucanas lay colored eggs."

"Wait a minute," I said. "You're drooling. I can't believe this. They're *chickens*."

Melissa spent her days walking farm after farm helping farmers deal with soil and water erosion problems, and quickly discovered a deep kinship with these independent men and women who worked so closely with the soil, with animals, and she couldn't stop talking about it.

"I saw the sweetest Jersey cows today," she said one day. Another day she came home and dropped the county map into my lap. "You have to see this part of the county—the hills are beautiful." She bought a poster that illustrated forty-two cattle breeds.

When you live in a small Minnesota town, you can't drive anywhere outside that town without passing a farm. As Melissa raced down Highway 52, she pointed to a pasture near the road. "See those black and white cows? They're Belted Galloways, but people call them Oreo cows." The car drifted over the white line onto the shoulder and we hit the rumble strip. *Rumble, rumble.* "Oh, sorry."

Five minutes later. "Look! Toulouse geese! I saw them in the catalog." I rolled my eyes, which did no good because she didn't notice. Five minutes later. "Whoa! Check out the size of that tractor." *Rumble, rumble.* "Oh, sorry."

"Excuse me, dear, but are you, like, paying *any* attention to the road?" Somehow, after eleven years, I'd actually developed that irritating voice spouses use to needle one another, which disappointed me because I thought, as a lesbian, I'd somehow be better at relationships than heterosexuals.

"Look at those sheep," Melissa said. "Don't they look peaceful?" *Rumble, rumble.*

"Yes, now may I drive?"

I should have realized what the future held the day I looked up and caught her giving me a dreamy look from across the kitchen table. Touched, I reached over and took her hand in mine. She squeezed it gently, and said, "God, I love chickens."

But I still didn't see it coming. One Saturday afternoon, after we raked the leaves and bought the fixings for homemade pizza, I started revising yet another story. My editor was interested in seeing more manuscripts. Story ideas stacked up in my head like planes over a fogged-in airport.

Melissa had inherited a small amount of money from her namesake, her great-aunt Melissa. "We could use the money to buy land," Melissa said, talking to me as I tried to work.

"Why would we do that?" I asked.

Melissa hesitated, then plunged ahead. "I've always wanted to be a farmer."

I looked up and put down my pencil. "You didn't put that in your personal ad."

"I know. . . . Would you help me?"

"What kind of farm?"

"I don't know. We'd have to find some land first, then go from there."

My mother's parents had had a sheep ranch in Montana, which my grandmother ran by herself after my grandfather died. I'd grown up visiting the ranch about once a year, and as a child could not even begin to appreciate how hard my grandmother worked. Because my Uncle Kenny and Aunt Ilene farmed in eastern North Dakota, and my Uncle Albert had ranched in Montana before his fatal construction accident, farming wasn't totally foreign to me. Melissa's grandparents had farmed in southern Illinois, raising beef cattle and mules in the days before tractors.

Melissa had been incredibly supportive as I wrote. I'd been contributing only my pathetic paychecks from odd part-time jobs to the family income, instead of the technical-writer salary I could earn if I knocked on IBM's door twenty minutes away in Rochester.

Farm? Me? Anyone reading the papers knew farms were a dying way of life, most agriculture shifting to large, factory operations as farmers either got bigger or got out. Also, Minnesota's rural population was rising, but the number of farmers was decreasing as people fled the suburbs, buying up farmland and letting it sit fallow, basically turning farmland into a big backyard, or perhaps renting the land to a nearby farmer, but not farming themselves. Getting into farming now would be like climbing up onto the *Titanic* while everyone else was throwing themselves off the ship.

For a few days I thought about Melissa's idea a lot. I loved planning things. I loved organizing. I loved researching. If we started a farm, I'd get to do all three. Maybe we could even buy a few books on farming. A few years earlier, after I'd quit technical writing, I worked in several bookstores, and I nearly went broke. Bookstore employees often get a 40 percent discount on books, so if you work in a bookstore for minimum wage, your paycheck buys books. For months I stashed bags of new books in all our closets so Melissa wouldn't know what I was up to.

I considered Melissa's plan. "If we start a farm, can we buy books on farming?"

"Absolutely. *Lots* of them."

Except for a few romantic tendencies, I believed I had my feet firmly planted on the ground. My parents raised me to be self-confident, which I am. They raised me to take care of myself, which I can. They raised me to think before I act, which I do ... usually. But I could have thought and read for years, and still not have understood *really* what lay ahead.

Partners should support each other's dreams. Besides, what could be more romantic than living in the country and writing? "Let's start a farm," I said.

She gave me a kiss. "Best twenty-one bucks I ever spent." (The price of a personal ad in 1983.)

baby on our doorstep

i **didn't want** to be more than ten minutes from our town's library, so this narrowed our options. There was surprisingly little farmland for sale. The newspaper listed either huge farms of 250 acres with grain bins, dairy barn and silos, or the 10-acre hobby farm, great for a few horses but not much else unless you were growing vegetables. We kept looking, and one day I saw a small For Sale sign at the edge of a hilly field next to the major four-lane highway running from the Twin Cities to Rochester.

The real estate agent took us for a tour. The size was great—fifty-three acres, and it was only five minutes from my library. Aside from that, the list of pros paled beside the list of cons. No buildings, no house, no fence, terrible soil quality, severe soil erosion. No one in their right mind wanted it, except, of course, my love, the soil conservationist. "It's like someone abandoning a baby on our doorstep," she pleaded. "It needs us."

Parts were too hilly, parts were too close to that noisy highway. Two inches below the surface lay green clay so dense I could form *pots,* for God's sake. A pathetic little creek ran through snarls of willow trees. We would have to build a house on the edge of the field—no trees nearby, a lonely thought for someone raised in a yard with over seventy-five oaks.

"This is likely where we'll live for the rest of our lives," I said.

"Won't it be great?" Melissa hugged me.

"But I'd always thought I'd end up living by water, maybe by the ocean." I craved water, a Pisces through and through.

Melissa swept out her arms. "Look at the grass in that pasture." The breeze rippled through the lush, green pasture in waves. "And there's water here—you can visit the creek anytime."

"Honey, that creek is two feet wide, and about one foot deep."

"Hey, it's water!"

We loved being on the water together. For much of our relationship we'd clear off as many weekends we could to throw the canoe onto our Trooper and go camping. Our first several canoeing experiences, however, had been about as pleasant as a ruptured appendix. Melissa had learned to canoe at camp, and while I found it easy to pick up, we spent most of the first few trips snapping at one another. Finally Melissa figured it out and found the perfect metaphor for me.

"We can't have two Captain Kirks in the canoe."

"What?"

She pointed to the stern. "Captain Kirk sits here. He steers. He's in charge." I didn't yet know how to steer, but hadn't let that stop me from trying to direct the canoe from the bow. She pointed to the bow. "Mr. Spock sits here. He follows the captain's orders." The fine art of canoeing suddenly made sense, and we soon took turns being Captain Kirk and Mr. Spock in the canoe.

As we considered buying this farmland, Melissa's optimism and energy were contagious. I began to see the farm through her eyes, and started liking what I saw. An unfamiliar awe spread through me as I stood on the highest spot and realized we could actually *own* this land. I could walk across it anytime I wanted. We could do anything with it. And with fifty-three acres, and trees, and privacy, perhaps

Melissa and I could even hold hands now and then, put our arms around each other, actually hug *outside*. Heterosexuals take touching for granted, but no matter where I'd gone, big city or small town, I had tasted people's sharp displeasure when I touched Melissa's shoulder in public or pressed too closely against her. We'd gotten so used to only touching in private we probably appeared more like sisters than lovers to the rest of the world.

We bought the land with Aunt Melissa's money. The land had no house, no barn, no outbuildings, no driveway, no fences. Our "baby left on the doorstep" had been abused and overfarmed for years, the soil depleted beyond belief. No earthworms crawled through the dense clay, driven away by years of chemical herbicide application.

We started getting to know our property with endless walks. Melissa dug a soil sample from the upper field. The silt loam was light brown because the nutrients had been totally leached from the soil. The blacker the soil, the more nutrients present. Another shovelful and she hit that green clay. Down the hill, toward the shallow creek, the soil was black and loose and fertile. Thanks to soil erosion, all the topsoil from the upper field ended up down here, where it was too wet to safely drive a tractor. We'd have to use the land as pasture, harvesting the grass with grazing animals.

As we walked, Melissa saw possibilities everywhere, while I saw only tall grass that hid bloodthirsty wood ticks just waiting for my tender flesh. The nameless creek running through the bottom of the pasture intrigued us both, but probably couldn't be used to generate income. Its banks were lined with long grass and snags of collapsing willows. Hard rains turned this narrow thread of peace into a raging forty-foot wide flume, exposing a new crop of limestone fossils each spring. The fossilized shells, coral, and cephalopods were Melissa's idea of buried treasure. I loved to find mini-waterfalls and listen to the hollow sounds as the creek fell only a few inches into the pool below.

Not counting the soggy land lining the creek, we had about forty-five acres of potential pasture, five acres of woods, and three acres for the house and future barns. This was about a zillion times more land than I'd ever owned in my life, and I struggled to get my mind around fifty-three acres, knowing it likely needed the same care and attention that our tiny townhouse yard had demanded. My world, once neatly contained in an urban or small town yard, suddenly stretched out paper-thin over fifty-three acres, which is about the size of fifty-one football fields.

The plan was to start the farm slowly over five years, then perhaps build a house and move. But the interest rates were so low Melissa's banker brother urged us to build right away. So early spring of 1994, we broke ground. We built a small home with a high, peaked roof and a loft. We were not the type of people to buy a lake cabin and drive two hours every summer weekend, so our home would be our vacation spot. Even though someone else did most of the work, the process consumed our lives.

Three carpenters, Jerry, Dan, and Kyle, built our home from the ground up with their hands and their brains, and I was overwhelmed with gratitude. We visited the site nearly every evening, picking up trash and dropped nails. Now and then we'd leave three giant candy bars on a window ledge for them to find the next day. Jerry ran a relaxed ship, and the two young men working with him were always polite and friendly. One particularly cold and windy day, I brought them two large pizzas so they'd have something warm for lunch. The four of us sat in what was to be our bedroom, and the men were clearly grateful for the pizza. As we talked, Jerry's gaze traveled around the room, constantly checking the work. He stopped, then calmly said, "Kyle, did you install that window there?" Kyle nodded, mouth full of pepperoni pizza. "Well, you might want to have another go at it. It's upside down." Sure enough, the window's lower crank was way up near the ceiling. Another carpenter might have railed at poor Kyle for putting a window in upside down, but not Jerry. We stared silently at the window for a second, then began to chuckle. Kyle grinned, flushed, and thought he might just turn that window upside right after lunch. I like to think that these men left some of their calm, gentle energy inside our house's framing.

With the help of both our families and lots of friends, we stained the cedar siding before the carpenters put it up. It was so orange everyone winced when they looked at it. Jerry assured us it would mellow to a nice warm color, then eventually turn silver. When the house was completed, we said goodbye to Jerry, and I think all three of us were on the verge of tears, surprised by how close we'd become as he and the two younger men had created our home.

On the hottest day of July, we moved in and fell in love with the house. The basement was unfinished to save money, and we planned to do that work ourselves over the next few winters. Amber and Tory were in dog heaven. They ran until their tongues hung out, stalked sparrows, and chewed on dead animals they found in the tall grass. Melissa was just as thrilled, and joined the dogs in all their activities, except the chewing-on-dead-animals part.

And me? It had never occurred to me there wouldn't be street-lights in the country. Outside, at night, it was so dark just inches in front of my face I would forget to breathe. The coyotes howling down the valley sent shivers down my arms. The owl sitting on our roof one night, softly hooting as she watched for prey, was lovely, but in a flash of intuition I couldn't help but imagine the lovely streak of manure she was depositing on our nice new roof. I should have asked myself if a glass-is-half-empty kind of person belonged on a farm.

wild hairs

i created an office in the corner of the unfinished basement, where gray concrete walls and floors absorbed all the light from the three windows in my corner. Spiders soon established an impressive network of sticky webs. The mice used my desk, an unfinished door suspended over two short file cabinets, as a playground, leaving little black turds sprinkled across my manuscripts. Everyone's a critic.

Dust from the exposed trusses above me showered my desk, and I soon realized I could save the expense of pens and pencils by simply writing with my finger in the thick gray-brown deposits. At least I was writing.

Six months later the USDA, in a frenzy of budget cutbacks, eliminated Melissa's position, so she found a part-time job, and our plans to farm shifted into high gear. Melissa dug through my office until she found a new manila folder. In her small, slanting print she labeled the folder "Wild Hairs," then stuffed in a few brochures and notes she had collected. The expression "She's got a wild hair up her ass" may have been a bit disgusting, but it certainly captured the crazy direction in which we were headed. "Okay," she said, "whenever we get an idea about how to make money on this farm, we put it in this file."

"Any idea?"

"No matter how crazy," she said.

I pulled a brochure from the bottom of a messy stack of mail on my desk. "I sent away for this last week. I think alpacas would be great." Cousins to the llama, the alpaca was shorter, but grew the highest quality hair of any of the camelid family. I was intrigued that alpacas were so biddable you could train them to climb into your station wagon, lie down, and ride that way. We wouldn't need a trailer or anything. We wouldn't have to eat the animals.

"Says here they can get pregnant again right after they deliver their babies, which are called crias," I said.

"How much do they cost?"

"The wool is the best in the world—a huge market for alpaca fiber."

"How much do they cost?"

"Well ... ahh ... breeding females cost about fifteen thousand dollars."

"Apiece?" Melissa squeaked. I put the alpaca brochure in the back of the file.

The Wild Hair file grew as we collected brochures, read books and magazines, attended fairs, meetings, and field days. We were sponges. The animals that we could graze in our pasture included: beef cattle, dairy cattle, hogs, sheep, buffalo, llamas, alpacas, goats, elk, red deer, ostriches, emus, chickens, and turkeys.

We looked at crops. Everyone around us raised corn and soybeans. But you needed great tracts of land to make any money— our fifty-three acres was too pathetic for corn and beans. But we could plant: shallots, garlic, shiitake mushrooms, vegetables, ornamental grasses, dried flowers, cut flowers, grapes, herbs, ginseng, pumpkins, and bittersweet.

While we explored farming possibilities, my career as an author kicked into gear. My first two children's books came out that year. *My Head is Full of Colors* was about a girl who, in an effort to figure herself out, one day imagines her hair is full of color, another day full of animals, then people and books. Illustrated by Kiki, the book was bright, colorful, and filled me with pride.

The Sawfin Stickleback: A Very Fishy Story recounted my first ice fishing experience, when, frozen with fear, I reeled in what felt like a monster fish, but in reality was only three inches long. The illustrator, Dan Yaccarino, drew wild fish guaranteed to make any child squeal.

Writing books for children leads to requests to speak at schools, where an author gives a presentation over and over again to kids grouped by age. My first request for a school visit came from a nearby elementary school. Would I be willing to speak to each grade?

Until this point I had structured my boundaries so public speaking was *outside* my life; I suffered from the classic fear of standing before an audience and opening my mouth.

The morning of the school visit I couldn't eat. As I drove to the school, the steering wheel trembled under my hands. When I found myself in front of twenty second-graders, it didn't matter that they were happy to see me because they were missing Arithmetic. It didn't matter that they were excited to meet an actual author. All that mattered were the white dots of fear filling my vision.

I somehow survived the day, but knew that without help, I'd never take on another school visit, even though they paid well. So I joined a local Toastmasters club, and began showing up every Friday morning at six thirty to embarrass and humiliate myself. But the group wouldn't let me. Supportive and encouraging, they soon taught me I could speak without fearing loss of bladder control, without making myself sick. Buoyed up by their confidence, I launched myself on an auxiliary career—reading my books to children and hopefully inspiring them to write down their own stories. On school visits I picked up every germ known to the modern world. Kids would gather around me ("Touch my new spiky hair!" "Can I hold your hand?") and innocently infect me with colds, flu, and other scary things, like the case of mono that kept me weak and feeble for two months. Speaking to children became something more than a "wild hair" in my life. I earned good money, felt like a real author, and while the process exhausted me, I did enjoy talking with kids and getting them excited about reading.

Over the months I wrote, spoke to schools, got sick, recovered, all while Melissa and I thinned out the Wild Hairs file. I visited a friend's cattle. The massive black and white beasts stared at me as we walked into their pasture. Torn between curiosity and fear, the young steers, probably seven hundred pounds each, held their ground as long as they dared, then finally whirled and ran. I was stunned. Cows ran? If those gigantic animals were going to move, and move quickly, then forget it. Beef cattle were out.

"Dairy," Melissa said. "We could milk cows or goats or sheep."

"And when do dairy farmers get a day off?"

"They have to milk the animals twice a day, every day, all year long."

"And when do dairy farmers get a vacation?"

Melissa crossed that one off the list. We considered hogs, but hog manure could take your breath away—literally. Melissa's nose could read the breeze. During summer drives with the windows open, she'd sniff the air. "Cows." A few miles later she'd sniff again. "Hogs over on that farm." I rolled up my window.

Buffalo were too big. Elk were fascinating because the farmers just harvested their antlers and sold them for a ridiculous price in the Orient as an aphrodisiac. Clever marketing idea, but the elk and their high fencing were too expensive. The red deer market was too new, ostriches too mean, emus too foreign. That left goats and sheep and chickens.

"What about goats?" Melissa said. Our friend Mary, who lived about fifteen minutes away, raised goats and sold wonderful goat cheese, and she'd told us there was a market for the meat as well. With both goats and sheep, farmers breed the adult animals, raise the resulting kids or lambs to a certain age, then sell them for meat. The adults breed again, and the cycle starts over.

Early spring, when the threat of a snowstorm still hung in the cool air, Melissa and I headed over to Mary's to visit the kids born that week. Inside the warm barn, dozens of goats bleated as we headed for the kid pen. Baby goats are, by far, the cutest mammal babies ever born. Forget kittens and puppies, who are totally helpless for days afterwards. Goat kids come out raring to go, only needing an hour or so to get their bearings. After that, it's explore, explore, explore. Melissa discovered that when she dropped to her knees and bent forward, her back became an irresistible mountain for the week-old kids. She laughed as the goats climbed on her, pushing each other for the high spot, then sliding off onto her head. They leapt and twisted, jumping up on us like puppies, sucking on our fingers and coats and bootlaces.

On this we both agreed—even though the animals we would sell for meat would be adult-sized, goats were just too gregarious for a meat-based operation, especially one started by overly tenderhearted farmers.

That left sheep. Visit a goat farm, and the kids come running to meet you. Visit a sheep farm, and the lambs run away. We wouldn't become buddies, so the selling would be easier; sheep were small, relatively inexpensive, and supposedly easy to manage. And the meat known as "lamb" wasn't, in fact, those cute little babies running away from us, but sheep who were eight to twelve months old and nearly as large as adult sheep. I felt better already. We would make babies, raise them to 60–70 pounds, then sell them to another farmer who would "finish" them, or feed them up to market size of 120 pounds. We would keep a few to finish ourselves, and gulp—eventually eat.

Now for the crop. Nothing looked right until Melissa read an article about Minnesota wineries needing more Minnesota-grown grapes. We researched grapes. We had the perfect spot. Because the land sloped to the south, water could run off and vines would have southern exposure. Our steady breeze would cut down on diseases caused by too much moisture. The soil, of course, was crap, but the winemaker didn't care. "Grapes grow in anything," he said. We signed a contract—they would provide us with the vines, we would sell grapes to them for seven years, and they'd deduct the value of the vines from our first crop.

Grapes used to be a huge business in Minnesota until the grape industry in California established itself and trains began flooding Minnesota with California grapes. The Minnesota grape industry died, and the vines along with it. Not until the mid-1980s did interested growers and the University begin developing vines that could produce good wine and withstand the winter temperatures in Minnesota, which can easily reach thirty below zero.

Our massive Wild Hairs file narrowed to raising sheep on pasture, growing wine grapes, and raising chickens on pasture. It would take nine weeks to raise broiler chickens. How would it feel to then pay someone to butcher those chickens? No matter—I would think about that later. It would take about nine months to raise a lamb. How would it feel to then pay someone to butcher those lambs? Later.

It would take four years to establish the vineyard, then we could start taking off a crop. How would the two of us harvest an entire acre of grapes? Later.

Melissa had found a job at the local vet clinic, and I continued to visit schools and attend my writing groups and submit my manuscripts to editors. We never really stopped to consider the idea of time, and how starting a farm would fit into our already busy lives.

"Sheep, chickens, and grapes," I said. "Can we do this?"

"Of course," Melissa said. "We'll do fine. You keep writing children's books. I'll do the chores. It'll be great."

I liked the sound of that—the farm on one side of the fence, contained and under control, my writing on the other side, safe and secure. Yup. This writer's boundaries were *intact,* baby. Nothing to worry about.

even my *bra*
was more supportive

i have been blessed with a solid family, and a boring childhood. No sexual abuse. No verbal abuse, no poverty, no alcoholism, no drug addictions, no violence, no trauma, except for the time my dad pulled over the station wagon on our trip through Pennsylvania and threatened to spank my sister and me because we wouldn't stop picking on each other. No, Beaver Cleaver had more woes than I did.

There was, of course, the time when I was three, my infant sister had colic, and my mom was so sleep-deprived that when I did something uncharacteristically naughty she clutched my shoulders and started scolding me. I hauled off and slapped her. We were both so stunned she never grabbed me, and I never slapped her, again. My mother could make a family celebration out of anything, cookies out of anything, and showed me women could have a life outside the home when she returned to work when I turned eleven. She also taught me to clean my own bathroom, an affront to any healthy teenager, but a skill I now appreciate.

My father is a lifelong Republican, so when I became a teen I automatically considered myself a Democrat. We'd have heated dinner-table discussions about Nixon, about civil rights, about

Vietnam, about economics, and when I'd eventually box him into a corner with my unrelenting attacks, he'd beam with pride.

My sister, Sandy, three years younger, who is now an articulate and successful businesswoman, was a scrappy tomboy who took great joy in wrestling her gangly sister to the ground. I think she even bit me when she was five. She developed effective ways to cope with a sister who always read. On long car rides she'd ask me to sing with her, and I'd refuse, my nose buried in the latest Nancy Drew. She'd then stare out the window as if pouting, and start singing anyway, either off-key or messing up the words so badly I couldn't tune her out.

"That's not right," I'd snap. "It's 'She'll be coming around the mountain when she comes,' not when she *drums*."

"Really?" Soon my book would be closed and we'd be singing "Love Potion No. 9" at the top of our lungs.

Even though my family was usually close and supportive, doubt fluttered through my gut when it was time to tell them I was going to be a farmer. My parents had divorced ten years earlier, so I faced two conversations.

I sat down with my mom in Wisconsin. "Mom," I said, "we are going to start farming. We're going to raise sheep."

"Farm?" Mom squeaked. "You?"

"Yes, me," I replied, confused and just a little defensive. "I thought you'd be happy I'm following in Grandma's footsteps."

She removed her glasses, rubbing her eyes. "Farming is hard work."

"I know. We have everything planned out."

"You're thirty-eight."

At thirty-eight, my mother had had a husband and two teenaged daughters, ran a house, worked full-time, belonged to professional associations, developed gardens all around our house, and sewed her own clothes. I could certainly handle a few animals.

I rolled my eyes and visited my accountant father in Minnesota. "Dad, we're going to start a farm."

Two eyebrows raised in alarm above thick glasses. "Is that really a good idea?" This from the man who'd supported every career move I'd ever made? Who was happy for me as long as I paid my bills on time, changed my engine oil every three thousand miles, and reconciled my bank statements regularly?

What was the big deal? I had wanted to be an economist, so I became one. I had wanted to be a writer, so I became one. Melissa needed help starting the farm, so I would become a farmer. I'd hadn't failed at much in my life so far, mainly because I never attempted anything I didn't already know I could do. Taking risks isn't something a control freak really gets into.

When I'd come out to my parents years ago, they'd been upset and concerned, but had eventually gotten used to the idea, and were very cool. But now, my news was almost more earth shattering. Being a lesbian was one thing, but being a *farmer?* Man, oh man, that was going to take some getting used to.

When I called my sister, who had fled the winters to live in Florida, she just laughed and laughed until she realized I was serious. I could hear her thinking, wasn't being gay odd enough? Besides, she'd been the active outdoor child, not me.

My extended family is small. I only have six aunts and uncles, and six cousins, so we are close, and see each other every opportunity we get. I'd never formally "come out" to any of them, but when I had presented Melissa to the family, they'd opened their arms and welcomed her in.

My doubts about farming, however, turned to stubbornness when I talked to these relatives. Aunt Ilene and Uncle Kenny, on my father's side, farmed the lush, black dirt of the Red River Valley in eastern North Dakota, and while visiting, I told my cattle-raising uncle that Melissa and I were going to start a farm. "You're kidding," he said.

"Sheep. We're going to raise sheep," I said bravely, knowing cattlemen abhor sheep.

He shook his head, wincing. "You know what they say." I waited, suspicious of the teasing smile spreading across his wide, friendly face. "The only thing dumber than a sheep is the farmer who raises 'em."

Oh, for heaven's sake. When I called Byron, my truck driver/cattle rancher cousin in Montana, this time on my mother's side, I told him the same thing. Silence on the phone, then, "Are you crazy?"

Cripes. What was *with* my family? "We're going to raise sheep," I said.

I held the phone away from my ear as deep guffaws blasted out the receiver. When Byron finally regained control, probably wiping away tears of mirth, he chuckled and cleared his throat. "Hey, what's the only thing dumber than a sheep?"

Okay. That was *it*. They thought they knew me. They thought I was just a pathetic bookworm. I was much more than that. I was strong. I was tough. I was a problem solver. I was a lesbian, damn it. I'd show them.

a paper farm

i studied our poster of sheep breeds, poring over the photos and characteristics of the Dorset, the Corriedale, the Hampshire. Sheep seemed to fall into three categories: white-faced, black-faced, and exotic. The white-faced all looked alike to me. The black-faced all looked alike to me. The exotic Jacobs's horns twirled out from its head. Cotswold had thick curly hair that hung in its eyes. The Merino's fine wool flowed like milky water, almost touching the ground. Polled Dorsets were big and meaty. Few sheep had the dramatic curled horns associated with rams. Polled, or hornless, sheep were more popular with shepherds, for obvious reasons.

I walked through the sheep building at the Minnesota State Fair with Mary, who, as a goat farmer and cheesemaker, knew little about sheep but decided to test me. She pointed to a white-faced ewe. "What breed is that?"

"Rambouillet," I said without hesitation.

"And that one in the next stall?"

"Targhee."

Mary stopped. "I am impressed. You've really learned your stuff."

I pointed above our heads, out of my shorter friend's range of vision. "Those signs above each stall really help."

We joined the Southeast Minnesota Sheep Producers Association (SEMSPA), a loosely run group of friendly shepherds, and the members opened their arms and took us in, not even blinking an eye that two women were farming together. They were thrilled someone actually wanted to get into sheep rather than *out* of sheep. It gets lonely on a sinking ship, so it's nice to have new faces show up.

As we studied sheep, I started a new job teaching writing through a ten-assignment correspondence course, which taught adults how to write for children. It was a well-paying job, and I didn't have to leave the house. Once a week the nice UPS man delivered a packet of student assignments. I had one week to critique them, writing each student a letter with advice and suggestions, then put the whole package in my mailbox. One friend, an experienced writer and teacher, had told me the job would affect my creativity, that spending my days reading other people's stories would diffuse my need to write my own. Poppycock.

I sold a third book to my editor, this one about why the sun and moon could sometimes be seen in the sky together. I started working on a middle-grade novel, and won a year-long mentorship working with Marion Dane Bauer, a highly-respected children's author.

Writers need energy to market their work. Rejection is a constant in the publishing world so writers must, when receiving a rejection letter, turn right around and submit the manuscript somewhere else. You can't publish if your work never leaves your desk. This takes tremendous persistence, and can slowly chip away at your self-esteem if you let it.

The longer a writer goes between publications, the harder it is to believe in herself, partly because the public measures writing success by publication alone. When a writer identifies herself as such to a new acquaintance, the first question posed is *always,* "What have you published?" Not how many grants have you received, or what kinds of things do you enjoy writing, or where do you get your ideas? It's "What have you published?"

I shared this attitude. My first writing course had been with Marion, who asked us on the first day of class: "If you knew you would never be published, would you still write?" This whole pathetic group of wannabe writers bobbed their heads up and down, sure the True Path to Nirvana could only be found by writing for writing's sake, not for publishing. I kept my own opinion to myself, of course, but I thought, geez, people, get a life. At that time I was positive the only reason to write was to publish.

Maybe there was one other reason, and that was to stop the spiders from totally taking over my desk. I fought them constantly for control of my space, but even when I won, my "office" was such a dreary place I often fled to the living room, which didn't work well either. Melissa's theory was if I was visible, I was fair game for a conversation, and soon our discussions would switch from writing to farming. We studied *Raising Sheep the Modern Way,* by Paula Simmons. We read *An Introduction to Keeping Sheep* by Jane Upton, and *The Sheep Raiser's Manual* by William Kruesi. In *The Sheep Book,* author Ron Parker wrote that sheep were the ideal domesticated animal—hardy and healthy, endearing, with a quality that made them a symbol of rural peace and tranquility. Perfect.

Melissa and I visited farms where the sheep lived in barns. Flies buzzed around our heads as the smell of concentrated sheep manure burned my nostrils, but at least we got close enough to the sheep to touch their rock-hard heads, to feel their pink-white skin toasty warm under five inches of crimped fiber. Melissa dove right in to every situation, handling the sheep whenever possible, asking questions about machinery and pasture seed mix and feeding systems.

Most shepherds had their animals give birth, or *lamb,* in the barn in the middle of the winter. Winter lambing allowed a farmer to spread out her labor over the year so she'd be free for field work in the spring. Just before the ewe delivered, the farmer put her in a four-foot by four-foot pen, called a *jug,* to keep ewe and baby close so the maternal bond could develop. Apparently sheep had the reputation of being less than attentive mothers, actually walking away from their newborns. The shepherds did everything for the ewe, down to cleaning up the newborn and making sure it nursed. I shuddered at the thought of getting up every two hours at night to check on ewes in the dead of winter. Maybe sheep weren't such a good idea after all.

But then we visited farms where the sheep ranged on pasture, hardly ever seeing the inside of a barn. On Paul and Lela's farm, about fifteen miles away, everything happened outside on pasture. The ewes spread out, choose their own spot for giving birth, and they bonded with their lambs immediately. With this system the farmer had to wait until the weather warmed up—mid-May— before lambing. Paul charmed us with his booming voice and twinkling eyes, and we visited their place again, asking them questions nonstop.

I liked the idea of rotational grazing, which meant the sheep were moved from pasture to pasture nearly every day. With this method, the sheep had clean grass to eat, and they fertilized the entire farm as they grazed. Rotational grazing meant the sheep didn't have to live in a feedlot, crammed together, living in their own manure, and being fed grain, which is easier for a farmer to handle than grass or hay. Our research showed that ruminants, animals like sheep, cows, and goats, did better eating what their bodies were built to eat: grass. And the whole system seemed more sustainable. The animals would have a high-quality life, and we wouldn't have to spend hours every day inside a barn. Not only that, but things fell together more naturally outside; the ewes were better mothers. This was the "old-fashioned" way of doing things, the way my grandparents had done it most of their lives until the USDA convinced farmers in the mid-1950s that everything should be done in the barn.

I watched the placid animals bite the grass, amble a few steps, bite again, then lay down and chew their cud. We could handle these animals, no problem.

We joined a group of women farmers involved in sustainable agriculture because this approach clicked with us. At the time, the definition of a sustainable farm involved three pieces: economic— the farm needed to be successful in order to support the farmers; environmental—the farmer worked with Nature rather than against her, caring for the land rather than harming it; and quality of life—both for the farmers and for the animals.

I ran our projected income and expenses over and over again. Yes, we could make money at this. No, we wouldn't get rich. We bought more sheep books. We attended all the SEMSPA meetings, feeling like permanent wannabes because we still didn't have sheep. We made a huge map of what our farm would look like—fences, gates, water hydrants—and asked Paul and Lela to look for flaws in our plan.

"Good heavens," Paul boomed. "I've *never* seen anyone give so much thought to this before. You girls are going to do just fine. This is great, just great."

"We thought we'd winter the animals here, then move them into this pasture for lambing, then start rotating them all summer over here," Melissa said.

I slid my finger across the elaborate drawing. "We'll use this gate to load up the animals, and this gate to get the tractor in and out of the pens."

"Amazing," Paul crowed, "just amazing." Melissa and I exchanged a happy glance. Damn, we were good.

We decided to avoid purebreds, preferring the vigor that comes from crossbreeding. And we also didn't want to get into the fancy wool breeds because we were told that fine wool usually meant poor meat quality, and excellent meat quality often meant poor wool quality. Since the value of wool was basically in the toilet, thanks to Australia and New Zealand flooding the market, and more people wearing polar fleece than wool, wool wouldn't be our main business, only a by-product. We found Lee, a small, gray-haired woman with bright eyes who raised a successful mix of five breeds—Columbia, Corriedale, Targhee, Dorset, and Finn. This five-way cross of animals were good mothers, easy lambers, did well on pasture, and had plenty of milk. We would also buy two ram lambs from her with Texel breeding—good meat producers.

"How many ewes should we buy?" I asked.

Melissa pulled out her notes from our sheep class. "Janet says it takes just as much work to raise ten as it does one hundred sheep."

"What?"

Sure enough, the numbers made sense. You needed fencing and gates for ten sheep. That same fence could enclose one hundred sheep without costing any more. You needed to feed and water and monitor ten sheep. It didn't take that much more time to feed and water one hundred. I swallowed hard. "I think one hundred is too many." The average flock in Minnesota was ten sheep. We'd go from being wannabes to being one of the largest flocks in the area. Besides, there were Melissa's headaches to consider. Would we be able to take care of all those sheep even though Melissa had a major headache about every other day? The year before we met, she'd hit an icy patch and rolled her Jeep. When she later began having headaches, no one could really find the cause. By now she'd tried lots of doctors, and a whole list of Eastern techniques—acupuncture, acupressure, herbs, you name it.

But the headaches persisted. Finally she found a physical therapist who told her something was wrong with a vertebra in her neck. It kept shifting out of position. He put it back, and life was good for a day or two, then it moved back.

Despite strengthening exercises and more doctors, the headaches continued. She had worked all those years as a soil conservationist with often debilitating pain, and couldn't bear the thought of an off-farm job where she couldn't stop if she felt sick. Pain made concentration difficult, but sheer stubbornness had kept her going, and Melissa was determined to do the same with farming—plow ahead regardless of the pain.

Headache or no headache, we argued back and forth about sheep numbers for days. In the past we'd argued about the color to paint the bathroom, or who forgot to replace the empty toilet paper roll, but the stakes had been fairly low since being wrong was only a matter of wounded pride. As I faced my uncertain future as a farmer, it suddenly seemed that being wrong would prove to be much more serious.

"What if we really screw up and they all die?" I'd never thought of myself as a doomsday person, but this seemed the opportune moment to become one. "What if you have too many headaches? What if we don't have enough pasture?"

Melissa countered with reassurance and facts, but I finally raised enough doubt in her mind that she agreed to a more reasonable entry into sheep. We would start with only fifty lambs, but at least we'd start. Melissa was itching to *be* a farmer, tired of just talking about it.

We agreed, without argument, that we would not, under any circumstances, name our sheep. *Real* farmers didn't name their sheep, and Paul said it was hard to eat something with a name. Instead, each animal would have a numbered ear tag. We attended a SEMSPA meeting and shared our plans with another shepherd. "Fifty ewe lambs?" Joe said. "*All* ewe lambs?"

"Yes," I said. "Is there a problem?" A female sheep under one year old was called a ewe lamb; a male was a ram lamb. Once they turned one year old, they become simply ewes and rams. We'd been told if you bought a flock of older ewes, you were likely buying someone's rejects, animals that no longer produced well, or that had health problems. Starting with ewe lambs gave you a fresh start at a good flock. We'd mapped everything out on our diagram. We'd run the numbers. Our paper farm looked great.

Joe shook his head. "Ewe lambs." He scratched an ear, making a face that sent my stomach lurching into my boots. "Well, you'll probably be okay." He caught the eye of another shepherd, whose eyes widened. "Yeah, it shouldn't be too bad." Uh oh.

shepherds at last

in the midst of our planning, Melissa's father, a retired psy-chiatrist who'd specialized in geriatrics, was diagnosed with Alzheimer's. Within a few months the family had to move him into a nursing home, and Melissa visited her mother nearly every week, helping her keep the house running and visiting her father.

Despite the added pressure, Melissa and I inched toward our goal to farm. Meanwhile, Mary tamed two of her goat kids to sell to a friend as pets, but the friend changed her mind, which left Mary with two neutered males. It's harder to take friendly animals to the butcher, but Mary had few options . . . except us.

"They need a home," Melissa said.

"But—"

"They could eat all the overgrown brush and clean up the old fence lines. Goats love that stuff."

"But—"

"They have names and everything. Lancelot and Merlin."

"But—"

"Here are some baby pictures Mary took when they were only hours old."

I glared at her. "No fair," I muttered as I looked through the pictures. We went to visit. When I sat down on a pile of rocks, little Lancelot promptly draped himself across my lap and fell asleep. Two weeks later, Lancelot and Merlin came to live on our farm.

The goats would rub against my legs, nibble my fingers searching for grain, and nicker whenever we appeared. They were like big dogs, only with horizontal pupils and four stomachs. An American Alpine, Lance's black and white hair shone. Merlin was an Oberhasli, a dark red-brown with black legs and a black strip down his spine. They were each about ninety pounds, and only came up to our knees, but they'd be close to two hundred pounds when full grown. I fell in love so fast it surprised even me.

I viewed the goats as a test, and since we managed to keep them alive without too much effort, we were ready for sheep. It was July, and we now had a house, a perimeter fence, two metal buildings, two goats, and no more money. The time had finally come to get up close and personal with ram testicles. We drove down to Lanesboro in our newly purchased farm truck, a 1987 gray Ford F-150 pickup with a really bad skin problem. Melissa was so proud of this ugly thing she practically puffed up as she drove. We had to sell my beloved Red Isuzu Trooper to pay for the pickup, so I was still pouting a little. We borrowed a friend's plywood racks to raise the sides of our pickup high enough to contain animals.

We were buying fifty ewe lambs from Lee, and two ram lambs. She raised hundreds of breeding lambs every year, and we were lucky to be able to buy from her. She had an old barn, one of those fascinating fading red structures I'd always seen from the highway but had rarely entered. Once inside the musty barn, I wrinkled my nose at the sharp smell of manure. Lee stood in the midst of forty ram lambs, born early that year, each lamb now weighing about sixty pounds.

"Take your pick," she said proudly, waving her arms toward the ram lambs. As we waded into the bunch, they bleated and ran for the corners of the pen. Ewes bellowed on the upper level. I sneezed at the dust the lambs raised. Melissa and I looked at each other and shrugged, so she dove into the pack of lambs and came up with a squirming, kicking ram lamb. I stepped back, wondering if there was some way to choose two ram lambs without actually touching them.

Melissa tipped the small animal back on his rump, and we bent over him.

"Not exactly sixteen inches, are they?" I whispered. Only six months old, this little guy's scrotum was the size of a squashed tangerine. We proceeded to choose two ram lambs, using scientific criteria like who had the cutest faces, and who Melissa could catch. Soon we had as many of the lambs, ewe and ram, as we could fit into the back of our pickup. We couldn't fit everyone, so Melissa would have to come back later for the rest of the ewe lambs.

"Are you sure those ram lambs won't mate with the ewe lambs?" I asked Lee. We had heard horror stories of rams jumping fences, rams mating through fences, causing all sorts of breeding havoc for shepherds. Some farmers had just given up and let the rams live full-time with their ewes, which meant the farmer never knew when the lambs would be born.

"No, they're too young to breed," Lee assured me. "Around September, though, when the weather starts to cool, that's when you'll need to be careful."

Even so, I spent the entire drive home peering through the back window of the cab, ready to leap through and cause coitus interruptus if those ram lambs got any romantic notions. There would be none of that hanky-panky on our farm. There would be absolutely no unauthorized sheep sex until December. None. Ever. *Never.* But the lambs just huddled together, scared and adorable. Our Columbia-Corriedale-Targhee-Dorset-Finn lambs were small, with sweet white faces, a few with topknots of shaggy wool, a few with speckled Koala bear faces. My pride took me by surprise, closing off my throat. Holy smokes. We were shepherds at last.

We backed the pickup to our new sheep pen, and opened the tailgate. Free, the animals leapt from the truck, ran thirty feet, then stopped to graze. We stood outside the pen, enchanted. We shooed the two ram lambs into their own paddock, where their sperm would be safely behind an eight-wire fence charged with 8,000 volts.

The ewe lambs grazed placidly, their stubby tails wagging now and then, their round bellies swaying as they walked. Serene pastoral scenes filled my mind. This was going to be a piece of cake.

wild woolies

melissa made another trip with the pickup to Lee's, so by the next day all fifty ewe lambs were on the farm, bought and paid for. Now it was time to move the ewe lambs from the pen out onto the pasture. Here's why my cattlemen relatives disliked sheep: when you try to move sheep, they don't move like cattle. So if they don't move like cattle, they must be dumb.

But our books said sheep aren't dumb; their actions make perfect sense for a small animal that large animals with sharp teeth want to eat. A farmer just can't expect a 150-pound sheep to act as calmly as a 1,000-pound cow that isn't afraid of much.

Sheep survive by being nervous, by flocking together hoping to intimidate a hungry coyote with their wall of white. They survive by running away. They survive by disguising any weaknesses, like being sick, so a predator won't pick them out of the flock as an easy victim.

The books said sheep just want to flee, so you must encourage them to flee in the right direction. This sounded easy enough.

Unfortunately these lambs had never seen a gate before, so there might as well have been a wall there instead. They ran past the gate, but would not go through it. "Circle around them again!" Melissa cried as she stood by the gate, hoping to show the ewe lambs where to go. I ran around one side of the bunched-up animals, pushing them toward the gate opening, which once again they ignored.

"Shit. Try it again," Melissa called. I did, pleased that I could keep up this level of aerobic exercise. The animals stampeded straight by the gate again.

Soon the sheep had worn a path in the grass, circling around the inside of the pen, running inches past the open gate. I had tripped on the rough ground at least twice, my knees hurt, and my heart rate indicated an attack was imminent. "You chase now," I panted.

But no luck. Finally the two of us, crouching down and waving our arms to look larger and more intimidating, got them bunched up right in front of the open gate. This is when I learned that if you violated a sheep's personal space, she wouldn't necessarily run away from you. She might run right *toward* you. Melissa and I pushed too close, and the sheep nearest us leapt into the air, wide-eyed, and shot right between us. The whole flock followed.

I began to understand Joe's concern about ewe lambs. There *was* a difference between ewes and ewe lambs. Picture women in a Tai Chi class, their controlled movements exuding calmness and serenity. Contrast this with a group of *fifty* fourth-grade girls who'd eaten nothing all day but Oreos, Hostess Twinkies, and sugar-sweetened Kool-Aid. And then show them three scary movies. Talk about jumpy.

Also, these animals could *move*. It took us an hour of running back and forth and screaming ourselves hoarse to get them through that gate. But when we finally succeeded, Melissa and I bent over, hands on knees, and struggled to breathe normally. "Border collie," Melissa gasped. I could only nod as I clutched my burning chest.

The next day we wanted to give these "placid" creatures vaccination shots. "C'mon, girls. Nothing to this!" Melissa called as we moved the sheep into a small holding pen, then single file into a narrow chute, where we could work on them one by one. The move went better than the day before because the lambs had learned that "gate" offered a means to get away from us.

The holding pen and narrow chute were part of our shiny new blue handling system, state of the art for shepherds. First we drove the sheep into a round pen, or tub, then we closed up an interior panel, squeezing them closer together so they'd "flee" into the narrow walkway, or chute. We would stand alongside this walkway to administer shots or inspect or do whatever mysterious sheep-related tasks awaited us in the future.

The salesman had assured us giving shots was easy and orderly with this handling system. Unfortunately the chute wasn't narrow enough for these little wild woolies—it was wide enough for mature ewes with lots of wool. A nervous lamb leapt into the air and came down facing the wrong way. "Turn her around!" Melissa cried, her hands busy with syringe and bottle. I bent over the sides of the chute and wrestled with the writhing lamb until she faced the right way. "Next," Melissa called, and the lamb popped into the air and came down facing backward again. My back burned.

Two of them must have been gazelles in sheep's clothing, for they sprang entirely over the three-foot high sides of the chute. "Which ones were they?" Melissa cried as we chased them straight into the sheep who'd already been medicated. They all looked alike. Clearly, we were going to have to record the ear tag number of each sheep as we inoculated her.

The afternoon dragged on. The sheep weren't tired, but we were. One lamb was backward, and I couldn't turn her around, so Melissa climbed into the chute and leaned over the lamb, who flew up and slammed into her face. "Shit! Ouch!" I inspected her nose to see if it'd broken, then together, we wrestled the wooly bundle of solid muscle until she faced the right way and could run through the chute.

One animal leapt over the sides of the chute into an empty pen.

"I'll get her," I called. "You keep working." I crouched in front of her. She lunged to her right so I lunged to my left. She put on the brakes and instead lunged to the left, but it was too late for me so I slammed into the ground. "Help," I muttered. We got her back in the right place, but three more thought this looked fun, so did the same thing. When I crouched in front of one of them, getting ready to lunge the wrong way, she jumped *over* my shoulder. Tiny cloven hooves whooshed by my ears as I fell to my knees. After a few hours of this my bruises had bruises.

Never having been one to swear, that afternoon I developed a healthy appreciation for the value of a good curse. *Gosh darn, shoot, good grief,* and *good heavens* just didn't cut it. Even my Norwegian grandmother's always useful *uff-da* failed me. Melissa had brothers, so she knew all the words. I learned them quickly.

Four hours later our blessed flock once again grazed peacefully. Melissa and I leaned against the barn, too exhausted to even walk back to the house.

"Well, that went well," Melissa said.

Too tired to speak, my brain spun. In five months, the middle of December, we were going to let the rams and ewes breed. Sheep sex meant that our flock of fifty sheep would turn into a flock of one hundred, at least. Was this really a good idea?

Melissa wouldn't let go of the border collie idea. While Tory was great at helping Melissa trap gophers, using her sensitive nose to find the best tunnels for placing traps, she couldn't run because she had horrible hip dysplasia, and Amber was too nervous. Besides, to herd sheep, you needed a sheep dog. So we made room in our hearts for one more dog and bought an eight-week-old border collie puppy and named him Robin. He was a tiny black and white bundle who hated to be cuddled, but loved to follow Tory around and play with her tail. Tory was patient with him, only snapping at him when his tireless energy finally wore her down. I knew how she felt. Some days I made Rob take a nap in his kennel just to get a break from his constant "play with me"; "throw this"; "okay, if you don't like that toy, throw this toy." The books did not explain that border collies do not have an off switch.

When he'd been with us for a month, he sat up in our front yard, really paid attention, and saw sheep for the first time. His genes kicked in, and the little black and white puppy dropped into a crouch. His eyes never left the sheep, and he began gliding forward, body as steady as a cat stalking a bird. Letting an untrained puppy in with sheep was a bad idea, so Melissa scooped him up and brought him in the house. But at least now we knew he had the border-collie eye, that steady gaze that could make sheep, or you, do anything the border collie wanted. When he was old enough to train, he'd be our secret weapon, the tool that would save us from having to run around in circles waving our arms and whooping at the sheep.

can't fit into
my grandma's genes

People got confused when they discovered neither Melissa nor I had grown up on farms. If you weren't born into farming, why on earth do it? An excellent question, the answer to which I wish I'd given more thought. Maybe farming genes skipped a generation, for our *grandparents* were farmers and ranchers.

We both liked the idea of returning to our roots, but did heritage make a difference? Was there a farming gene, one that would have made my life easier but that my parents had neglected to pass on to me? Somehow I doubted that just because my deceased grandparents raised sheep, I was any more capable of raising sheep than a woman plucked from the heart of New York City. This would prove, in fact, to be true.

My grandfather died of heart failure before my mother even married. My grandmother ran the sheep ranch by herself for years, and while I loved her, distance made a close relationship difficult. And because sheep were not part of my life while Grandma was alive, I didn't even think to ask her all the questions I now needed answers to.

So instead, my mom gave me stories. Stories about my grandfather Elmer LaRiviere, a descendent of the French LaRiviere who emigrated to Canada in the 1600s, and about my grandmother, Nora Wetherelt. Elmer had a terrible back, so at shearing time he'd string up a leather strap from the shed rafter, then hang over it, bent at the waist, to shear his share of the six hundred sheep. He was tough and gruff and expected the same of his children.

I never really understood myself what it meant to be French-Canadian until I watched the movie *Vertical Limit*. Two mountain climbers are chatting when the girlfriend of one of them walks by, glowering and snapping at him. He shrugs, then explains, "My girlfriend is French-Canadian. Most days she's Canadian, but today she's French." That explained a lot about my personality.

My French-Canadian grandfather spent days living in the sheep wagon, tending the sheep as they browsed for something green in the dry range at the far end of the two-thousand-acre ranch, a pitifully small spread for southeastern Montana. Time was heavy on his hands, so one summer he stitched, by hand, a little dress. As each daughter reached age four, my aunt, then my mother, and then my other aunt were each photographed in the precious dress, tiers of ruffled white muslin reaching down to dusty bare feet. This was the same man who held my grand-mother's hand in boiling water to punish her for "letting" one of their young daughters burn herself on the stove. This was the same man who, furious at a mean ram for knocking my grandmother down, grabbed an axe and nailed the ram right between the eyes. The ram shook his head, and left the barn unharmed, the dull axe doing no damage whatsoever. That's probably why Dodge likes to call its pickups "ram tough."

Widowed before I was born, my grandma was the toughest person I knew. During our hot summer visits to the ranch, she loaded my sister and me into her old white car, windows down for a breeze, and drove out to the pasture to check the sheep. She had little patience for her city granddaughters from the East as we shrieked at the huge grasshoppers that thwapped against the car ceiling and left juicy stains across our pleated shorts.

One summer she let Sandy and me care for a bottle lamb, whom we named Snowball. Grandma rolled her eyes and groaned. Now that we'd named her, Grandma couldn't sell her. Every summer we visited she'd point out Snowball, then Snowball's lamb Snowflake, and so on. She could have pointed to any ewe and pronounced her Snowball, but I don't think she did. Now that I had sheep of my own, I understood the burden we'd laid across Grandma's shoulders—it's hard to eat an animal with a name.

Mom began giving me more stories about Grandma, and they made me feel better. One day four of Grandma's sheep had gotten outside the fence. She tried to drive them back inside but couldn't. Sheep refuse to go where you want them to go, even if it's for their own good. Grandma finally went back to the ranch house, got her rifle, and shot all four of them. Freezer meat.

Stories connect us more deeply than any gift. That first summer, when one of those feisty ewe lambs faced me down, blindly determined to go the wrong way, I searched my depths for Grandma's farming genes, surely buried somewhere deep inside me. I gave the ewe my best icy stare, pointed a threatening finger directly at her, and said, as firmly as I could muster, "I *could* shoot you."

The wide-eyed animal snorted, then ran the wrong way. I hadn't inherited my grandmother's farming genes. I wished, however, that I'd inherited her rifle.

chicken run

Life in the country presented more distractions than I'd antic-ipated. Melissa would call down into my office. "Baltimore Oriole up in the caragana bushes," and I'd go look. A red-tailed hawk swooped low across our yard. Male pheasants honked from down along the creek. Towering cloud formations and dramatic thunderstorms drew me to the windows as well. My ability to focus on writing slipped a bit, but I was confident I'd regain it. Part of that confidence came from Melissa, who was my biggest fan, reading and critiquing everything I wrote.

In July, the same month we got the sheep, we also bought one hundred fifty baby chickens that we would raise for meat. They were hatched in a nursery in Iowa, plopped into a cardboard box with bedding and air holes, then shipped that day. Melissa brought them home from the local grain elevator the next day, and I instantly began worrying. They'd been without food or water for a day. How could they possibly survive?

Melissa calmly explained that just before a chick hatches from an egg, it takes into its belly the sac that contains the remaining yolk, so basically it's born with a full tummy. The place where the yolk enters the chick heals over, leaving a tiny scar.

"Like a belly button," Melissa said.

The news that chickens have belly buttons so astounded me I stopped worrying.

A cacophony of cheeping greeted me as I opened the chicken house door. One hundred and fifty yellow puffballs scooted across the floor, which Melissa had covered in newspaper so the new-borns wouldn't get confused and eat the wood shavings under-neath. Mesmerized, I watched them peck at the feed, sample the water, then suddenly race to the other side of the pen. When I clapped, the silence was instant. The chicks hunkered down, hop-ing to be invisible in the quiet.

Within a few days, the white pin feathers on their wings and tails began to appear, and soon the chicks looked as awkward as a teenager midway through his growth spurts. A few baby chicks died in our first batch. While we knew from our research that this might happen, the lifeless mound of yellow was still tough to see.

When they were three weeks old, we scampered around the chicken house scooping up the white chickens. Then we took them out to the pasture pens Melissa had built, two ten-foot by twelve-foot pens, two feet high, with wheels on one end, and an open bottom so the chickens could graze the grass. We moved the pens every day, giving the chickens fresh food and ground so they didn't have to live, day after day, in their own excrement.

This system was developed and promoted by an enterprising farmer from Virginia who raised thousands of chickens in these pens, moving the pens every day, creating such a booming busi-ness that he wrote a book and produced a video about it. We bought both the video, and of course, the book. A tiny part of me wondered if the guy made more money promoting his system than actually using it.

"You pick up the waterers, I'll get the feeders." Melissa lifted off the screened top to one corner of the pen and we pulled everything out—three wooden feeders Melissa had made, and two plastic waterers. I tried to avoid the white, runny manure, but it was nearly impossible. It was everywhere—wet, smelly, and sticking to my boots like glue.

We had one blind chicken that we lifted out of the pen every morning and set off to the side. Then Melissa lowered the wheels, lifting the back end of the pen off the ground. We each grabbed rope handles on the front end. By this time the chickens had all rushed to the front of the pen because they knew fresh food was only a few steps away. When Melissa shouted "Go!" I pulled, leaning into it as we wheeled the heavy pen twelve feet forward while the chickens clucked happily, walking along with the pen, a few laggards popping out behind the raised back. At fresh ground, I dropped the rope, looked into the pen to make sure no chickens were crouched under the raised end. "Down!" I shouted, and Melissa lowered the pen. One day we both checked, but didn't see the young chicken halfway under one of the other sides, so we unknowingly sat the pen down and broke her neck. I felt awful. "I couldn't see her from my angle," I said.

"I couldn't see her, either," Melissa shouted, now instantly on the defensive. But while we'd been arguing about more things these days, we both stared at the dead chicken, and silently agreed that pointing fingers would do no good. A dead chicken was a dead chicken.

We fed the chickens cracked corn every day and carried them fresh water daily, the heavy buckets bruising our thighs. We raised these birds from day-old balls of yellow fluff into huge plump chickens. Melissa talked to them every day, and I got into the habit myself. Chickens were kind of cute, actually, when you got past all their manure. They clucked and tipped their heads and were remarkably industrious. Then I looked at the calendar. The summer was slipping by too quickly. My editor had rejected several of my stories, and the one under contract wasn't going well because his requested revisions dragged me farther and farther from the story I had to tell. And worst of all, the chickens' butcher date was the end of August.

ménage à trois

at this point I realized that I now belonged to, or rather, participated in, a ménage à trois. Few can say this French phrase without waggling an eyebrow, winking, or wearing a sly leer. Somehow, adding a third party into a relationship heightened everything. A friend's French dictionary defined *ménage à trois* as simply, "a triangle."

The first member of this kinky triangle was me. Very tall, short brown hair, glasses, with what my mother called a Roman nose, a soothing term she invented to help soften the pain of living my adolescence as two long legs and a nose. At thirty-eight, my body had caught up with my nose, and then some. I was a sensitive Pisces, and would sooner read than breathe. My left brain constantly struggled to control the chaos my right brain craved. I was often anxious, but too controlled to show it.

The second member of the triangle was Melissa. A year younger, an inch shorter, thin, strong, with green eyes and thick hair that curled around her face and neck. Once on the farm, she took to wearing brown Carhartt work jeans with many pockets and a hammer loop. She was a stubborn Aries, and if she hadn't moved something or fixed something or done something, the day had been a waste. I suspected she broke things just so she had something to fix.

The third member in the ménage à trois was dark, earthy, and came to bed with us nearly every night. At fifty-three acres, the farm was by far the largest member of the triangle, the most demanding, and the one responsible for the bits of manure, hay, and straw left on my clean sheets.

Where did writing fit into this cozy little triangle? Perhaps my writing could provide a fourth point for a solid square, a neat little quartet.

Years ago an acquaintance had casually mentioned she and her husband had invited a third person into their relationship. I'd nodded, totally cool, but had in truth been totally shocked. Three parties in a bed? My head had spun, trying to work out the physical details, not to mention the emotional sand traps. Wouldn't someone eventually feel left out? Wouldn't someone get hurt?

I examined our ménage à trois. No, we would do things differently. We would pay attention and not let one part of the threesome mess up the relationship between the other two. It wasn't as if the farm rose like the flooding Mississippi and threatened to drown me. It wasn't as if the farm tried to kick me out of the house and steal Melissa for herself.

Besides, my relationship with Melissa was rock solid, and I couldn't conceive of anything threatening that, especially not a mere fifty-three acres of land.

a grape disaster

growing grapes in Minnesota was slowly beginning to take hold in the mid-1990s. We attended meetings of the Minnesota Grape Growers Association and soaked up as much information as we could. We studied grape varieties, trellising methods, diseases, weed control, and harvesting. Neither Melissa nor I liked the idea of using chemicals, so we decided we'd have a nearly organic vineyard. We wouldn't spray pesticides to keep off the bugs. We wouldn't spray herbicides, like Roundup, to kill the weeds. We'd spray organically approved products to help fight downy mildew. To keep the weeds down between rows, we would plant grass, and mow this with our old riding lawn mower. Weeds would spring up between the plants, which would be spaced four feet apart, but we would mow these as well. All we'd have to do is use our old push mower. Of course it would be tricky because a trellis wire would be running three feet off the ground, but we'd figure something out. Fools.

We hired a fencing company to build us a one-acre trellis for the grapevines. They used a tractor with a hydraulic post pounder mounted on the front, which literally pounded the ten-foot long posts four feet into the ground. They made eleven rows, each four hundred feet long. Then they strung two lines of wire, one three feet high, the other at six feet to support the vines.

Late spring we pulled together a crew of ten generous neighbors and friends, and we planted the first two hundred plants. These Frontenac grapes were a winter-hardy red-wine variety developed by the University of Minnesota and a group of grape growers. We'd chosen winter-hardy varieties because we didn't like the alternative. People raising more delicate vines must untie them every fall, lay them on the ground in trenches, cover them with straw, then tie them back up onto the trellis wires the next spring. Frontenac grapes were supposed to be hardy to thirty degrees below zero, so they could remain upright on the trellises and stand a good chance of surviving a Minnesota winter.

The vines had been started in a greenhouse, so were potted and about four inches tall. Our jolly crew dug holes, planted the vines, placed three-foot black plastic weed barriers around each vine and pinned them down. It was a stressful but amazing day.

The Frontenac grapes took four of the eleven rows. I planted one row of experimental grapes with bare roots a few days later. That left the remaining six rows for LaCrosse vines, a white grape. We were planting cuttings from existing LaCrosse vines made by another grower. The cuttings were only five inches long, with three buds on each, no roots, and a definite top and bottom. Once stuck bottom-down in the soil, the buds underground would become the roots. We had enough cuttings to plant two in each spot, hoping that at least one would survive.

Melissa had her hands full with tractor work getting ready for building construction. Planting the cuttings was something easy that I could do. Standard pruning practice was to make a diagonal cut on the top of the cutting, a horizontal cut for the bottom, so this was what I followed, sticking the horizontal cut end into the ground. My dad came to help one wet afternoon. "Are you sure this is the way they go?" he asked. Neither of us were gardeners.

"Of course," I said. "The bottom is cut straight across." We planted two entire rows, or two hundred vines.

A week later Melissa came in from checking on the vines. "Umm, I think the LaCrosse are planted upside down."

"That's impossible," I said, not because I didn't think I could make a mistake, but because the enormity of fixing it was just too huge to contemplate. Rain had fallen every day since I'd planted the sticks, turning the vineyard into a boot-sucking mire of clay.

Melissa called the grower who made the cuttings. "Yeah," he said, "I make my diagonal cut on the bottom of the twig so it'll slide into the ground easier when you plant them." No wonder the buds had appeared to be pointing downward rather than skyward. I *had* planted two hundred vines upside down. Imagine what a begonia would do if it was planted roots up. We spent hours sliding around on our knees in the mucky soil, turning the sticks upside-right.

"How long before you can laugh about this?" Melissa asked that night. She had forgiven me five minutes after she discovered my error, but I couldn't be as gracious with myself.

"Years." I actually slapped myself in the forehead every time I remembered. My stomach hurt for days. If I ever ran out of children's stories to tell, perhaps I could pen a useful handbook, *How Not to Farm.*

Some days it did, in fact, feel as if I'd run out of stories to tell, for not much happened in my dusty office. Perhaps my friend had been right—what if my teaching job was zapping my creative energy? I continued to submit stories I'd already written, so at least I was marketing my work, a task that requires brute persistence. Like all writers, I began accumulating an impressive collection of rejection letters. But at least I continued to succeed as an author, entertaining kids with my slide show. When another writer told me kids are hungry for information about the author as a person, I walked around the farm with my camera, capturing the sheep grazing, Lancelot the goat trying to climb inside the camera, and chickens pecking at corn.

While the grade-school children responded to the slides showing my books, they really engaged with the photos of the farm, and during my question-and-answer period many just couldn't hold back, telling me about their animals, or the animals on a relative's farm. Our livestock was sometimes a heavy weight on my shoulders, but when I visited schools, the animals proved to be a great connector between me and the children.

They liked me, they loved Lance, they loved the chickens, and were hungry for more about the farm.

Oh, and the upside-down vines? Of the two hundred replanted vines, eight would survive.

read the directions, dummy

One early August morning Melissa noticed many of the ewe lambs had messy back ends, wet manure caking the wool along the anus and down the legs. Gross. The vet tested a manure sample and found the sheep were suffering from coccidiosis. Not a life-threatening disease, but if left untreated it could weaken a sheep to the point of death. The books said sometimes the stress of moving to a new farm could cause a flare-up of coccidiosis.

We sprang into action. What were our options? The product of choice seemed to be Corid. The bottle said we had two options: (1) drench each sheep directly five days in a row, meaning squirt a mixture of Corid and water down her throat, or (2) add Corid to their drinking water for five days.

"Let's just add it to their drinking water. Sounds easier," I said hopefully.

"No, the drenching will be better. It should be more direct and fast-acting."

Damn. We rounded up the sheep into the handling pen, which took only half an hour this time instead of ninety minutes. When we finally corralled them, we began that bruising process of moving each through the chute, wrestling her onto her back end, and squirting the medication down her throat. After five uncooperative ewe lambs, we were exhausted, and we had forty-five left to go. Hours later, covered with dirt, sweat, and Corid, we collapsed onto the barn's gravel floor.

"Four more days of this?" I said.

"Hey, I have an idea," Melissa said, leaning against me, eyes twinkling. "Let's just add the Corid to their drinking water."

But after five days of Corid in the water, their back ends were still . . . messy. The pasture was littered with signs of diarrhea. Maybe another day of Corid would help. And another. And another. And another.

Eight days into our Corid treatment I heard terrified shouting outside. "Call the vet! Call the vet!" Melissa ran toward the house, a limp ewe lamb draped across her shoulders. She dropped to her knees in front of me and lowered the lamb onto the ground. Hands trembling, I dialed. Mark was on call, and lived less than a mile away. While we waited, the ewe arched her back, straining in a horrible convulsion.

Within minutes Mark roared up in his teal blue pickup outfitted with the huge white vet box, knelt by the lamb and frowned. "Looks like tetanus. They convulse like this with tetanus." Terror gripped both of us. Tetanus was deadly. The whole flock could be at risk.

He calmly asked questions as his hands probed the lamb's muscles. It didn't take long to get to the Corid. "How long have you been giving them Corid?"

We looked at each other. "Seven, eight days."

Mark hopped up and jogged to his truck, returning with a syringe filled with vitamin B. "The Corid dose should be only five days. Beyond this, Corid ties up the vitamin B in the sheep's body, and she suffers from a thiamin deficiency." He injected the vitamin

B into the lamb's neck. "These convulsions mean her nerves are starving for vitamin B."

In just a few minutes the lamb's tension eased a bit; she no longer arched her back so horribly. "Keep her quiet. Give her two more shots today, then put her back with the flock."

The flock. Visions of the remaining forty-nine sheep writhing on the pasture in thiamin-deficient seizures gripped both of us. "What about the others? Will this happen to them?"

"Maybe," Mark said. "Or maybe this lamb is weaker so she was hit first."

Melissa immediately gave the sheep fresh water without Corid. By evening the sick ewe lamb had recovered, and stood at the door of the pen, bleating sadly for her flock-mates. The next morning when we took her back, I held my breath as we surveyed the flock. Bite, rip, chew. Bite, rip, chew. The sheep grazed contentedly, no signs of seizures. What incredible luck. Without that first ewe, our "indicator" sheep, we might have killed the entire flock.

"You know, we're on the steepest part of the learning curve," Melissa said as we watched the lambs graze.

"Yeah, straight up."

The sheep recovered from their coccidiosis within a few days, so that was one disaster averted. But the fact that more likely waited to ambush us in the future injected a thin thread of tension between us. Not only were we life partners, we were now business partners as well, on a venture that neither of us really knew much about. To add to the tension, Melissa had recently helped move her father to another nursing home. With his sweater vest, distinguished handlebar mustache, and confident air, the retired doctor continued to "escape" from each nursing home because visitors entering would think he was a doctor and let him out. Once a state trooper found him wandering along the freeway.

We'd begun arguing more, but since the farm required us to

make more decisions, I guess that wasn't surprising. Worried about her father, Melissa was overworked and overwhelmed, but she thrived on caring for our animals. She was right where she wanted to be, right where she needed to be. But was I?

a shocking story

to control sheep you need fencing. Lots of it. So while the boundaries around my life were coming down, the fencing around the farm was going up. The first thing we needed was a perimeter fence, a big, super-charged baby that would keep an elephant in, or out. This was especially important because one side of our farm ran along the highway. Should our sheep get out of that perimeter fence and wander onto the highway, not only would they be killed, but we'd be liable for any damage or injury they caused.

The fencing company built the perimeter fence using five electrified wires, the top one as high as my chest. As long as the fence energizer worked properly, and always fed electricity to the fence, no sheep was going through that fence, for it kicked out almost 8,000 volts.

We also needed internal fencing to control where the sheep went and when. A sheep will pick out her favorite plants and eat them down to the ground. So we needed to move the sheep in small, controlled paddocks, forcing them to eat everything there instead of picking and choosing as if they were at a buffet. Just as I prefer pepperoni pizza to steak, the ewe lambs preferred bird's foot trefoil to orchard grass, red clover to white clover. We wanted them to eat it all.

So we broke our pastures into long, narrow runs about 140 feet wide. Each side of this run was enclosed by a three-wire electric fence. Then we ordered portable net electric fences, called Electronet, that were 150 feet long. We used these temporary fences, one in front of the flock, one in back, to enclose the sheep. Electronet had fiberglass posts every fifteen feet. Small wires were woven into the plastic net so the fence could be charged.

The first time I used the Electronet, the netting got all tangled in the posts and I wanted to scream. Then I took a deep breath and told myself this was happening to teach me patience. I eventually learned to hold the bundle of posts in one hand, and walk along, spreading out the fence. When it was all down, I retraced my steps, pushed the posts into the ground, pulled the fence tight so the sheep respected it, then hooked it to the three-wire fence so everything was "hot."

Every morning Melissa or I walked through the pasture, monitoring how short the sheep had taken the grass. When it was about six inches, it was time to move the animals. I set up another Electronet ahead of the sheep, smiling as the sheep gathered at the closed fence behind me, bleating for me to open it. They were finally starting to catch on to gates. I opened the fence, and hooves pounded as they ran for the fresh, tender pasture. I closed up the net behind them so they couldn't return to their favorite plants and overgraze. I liked to stand quietly, listening to the satisfying "crunch, crunch" of animals grazing. If my family could only see me now, I thought. Nothing to this farming stuff.

I struggled to understand electricity—the watts, volts, joules, the breakers, the switches, everything. But despite Melissa's constant coaching, the only thing I could grasp about electricity was that it hurt. Melissa refused to be cowed by this thing. She reached between the wires to tie something onto the post. When the ground was dry, she might touch the wire without much pain. But when she was kneeling in wet grass, she got such a jolt she fell back and stared stupidly at the sky. Once the fence burned a hole through her thick leather glove.

One afternoon she was weed-whacking under the fence. Too impatient to walk clear to the other side of the farm and turn off the fence, she waved this metal wand under the fence for hours. As she got tired, she had less control, and the machine's metal shaft touched the fence, conducting electricity straight up her arms. Unfortunately, as she reduced the quantity of weeds touching the fence, more voltage flowed through the fence. I was inside, trying to write, and heard a wild yelp every two minutes.

"A lot of folks would have turned off the fence," I said when she finally came in.

"Too much trouble. Did you hear me yelling? Wow, that was really something."

When an electrical current contacts your body, the first thing it wants to do is go somewhere, anywhere, and it's perfectly happy using your body to get there. If you're touching the ground, it wants to go to the ground, and if that means traveling through your muscles and bones to get there, no problem. If you're not touching the ground, the electricity has nowhere to go, so you don't feel it. That's why birds can sit on electric fences—the electricity has no place to go. So if you touch an electric fence, you're much better off if you aren't, at the same time, touching the ground. How you manage this without wings is not something I've been able to figure out.

I wisely respected the fence, but even I became complacent. Because the internal fences were only thirty inches tall, and my inseam was thirty-four, I soon stepped across the fences with brash confidence. But these fences ran parallel to the curve of the hills. When the level of the ground on the other side of the fence dropped even an inch, my four-inch clearance disappeared without warning. Ouch.

I finally got the hang of the ground-level thing and was more careful. At the time, I owned a pair of stretch jeans—not the height of fashion, but comfortable to work in. I felt slimmer wearing them, for they compressed my tender pink thighs to an almost-slender state. But I had worn these jeans so much—and those women with thighs will understand—that after a few months of farming I'd rubbed a large hole inside one thigh. My stretch jeans did a great compression job, except at the hole, where my tender pink thigh bulged out like rising bread dough. One day, wearing these jeans, I crossed the fence where I had crossed many times before. I always gripped the metal fence post to steady myself, and this time was no different.

But I failed to compensate for the extra inch of tender pink thigh. When that tender pink thigh hit the fence, the electricity surged up through my entire body and out the hand gripping the post, and my whole body spasmed in shock. I flung myself over the fence with a shout. Melissa came running and held me as I whimpered, then she generously shared her bag of M&Ms. I eventually stopped shaking and recovered, finally aware that I sat on the top of a grassy hill with sheep contentedly grazing below, sunshine warming my face, the lush valley stretching beyond, Melissa's arm around me. This farm adventure was proving more physically challenging than I'd expected, but at least we had each other.

to market, to market

the summer was a blur of moving chicken pens, building fences, rotating the sheep through the pastures to fresh grass every day, building shelves, buying tools, and mowing—the yard, the windbreak, the vineyard. Mowing, mowing, mowing. I never knew grass could grow so fast.

After a hot summer day outside in the fresh air, first mowing, then helping Melissa build fence, I struggled down into my office, swiping at the latest cobwebs, and sat down at my desk. My wind-burned face felt hot, tiny bits of cut grass scratched inside my sweaty t-shirt, shorts, and socks, and my butt ached from bouncing around on an old mower with bad springs.

I picked up my pen, opened a file, then lowered my head to my desk and moaned softly, grateful not to be moving. Eyes closed, I let my body relax and wondered which muscle group would ache most the next day. The pen dropped from my fingers. I would write tomorrow.

Tomorrow came. Chicken butcher date. Damn. This would be an emotionally exhausting day, so I likely wouldn't have much left for writing. As Melissa drove the pickup toward the chicken pens, I could tell from the set of her jaw this would not be easy for her either. I felt as if I were sliding down a steep, slippery slope—there was no way to stop the inevitable jolt at the bottom. An odd panic clutched my chest. Tomorrow morning these chickens would be dead. It was almost surreal. We had cared for these animals every day, and now we were going to pay someone to kill them. Then we would eat them.

Despite my anxieties, I did believe in what we were doing. Few people today have a clue where their meat comes from, just accepting that it's tightly wrapped in cellophane and comes from the grocery store. Few people remember this hard fact: that for them to eat meat, something had to die. But it's not just that an animal has to die—it's also how the animal lived. Many people simply don't connect the poor chicken raised in an airless, sunless building with the chicken on their plate.

I, too, had separated from my food, trying to forget I was eating animal flesh. Of the people who do face that directly, some swiftly become vegetarians. I tried that, but it didn't work. I hate to cook, and every single veggie dish I attempted flopped. Tofu is not my friend.

No, meat belonged in my diet. I knew that when we started the farm. We would raise chickens and lambs to sell. We wouldn't feed them growth hormones or antibiotics. We would raise them as naturally as possible. And then we would pay someone to kill them.

We removed part of the chicken pen's lid, then Melissa crawled inside the two-foot high pen, slipping on the wet manure and mud. On her hands and knees, she caught each bird and handed it, flapping and squawking, up to me. I put the chickens into crates that held ten birds, struggling to keep the wings down so they wouldn't hurt themselves, yet trying to save myself from their nail-sharp claws.

"This is too hard! Isn't there another way to do things?" I struggled to stuff another squawking chicken into a crate.

Melissa emerged from the pen, knees and gloves wet with manure, face red with exertion, hair sticking to her sweaty head.

"No!" She shot me a look of raw fury I hadn't seen before. I didn't know if it was me, the situation, or the pain of being so new at everything on the farm, but Melissa had devised a new stress-management tool: anger.

At that very moment I, too, was developing my own new management tool. This chicken business was chaos. I hated chaos. The only way to avoid chaos is to control everything around you. Of course, when an angry person is being controlled, she gets angrier. When a controlling person is faced with anger, she gets more controlling. Thus, early in the farm's operation, we set up our charming and unique pattern of business management.

But all my efforts to change the situation and control the chaos failed. There was just no other way to deal with these chickens, so we resumed the task.

After I put the chickens into the crates, they immediately quieted down. Finally the pens were empty, and our crates were full. In silence we loaded the heavy crates into the pickup and headed for the butcher. As she drove, Melissa returned to her usual cheery self. The sunset shot orange and purple across the building thunderclouds.

We arrived at dusk, the wind whipping up as a thunderstorm crashed overhead, the lightning flashing closer as we transferred the chickens from our crates to the butcher's crates. My arms stung with scratches from their claws. White manure splattered across my sweatshirt and down my overalls. Our birds sat quietly in the new crates, ready to sleep now that night had fallen. Tucked under a wide roof overhang, they would be protected from the storm.

The ride home was just as quiet, but I felt an odd mix of pride and relief. We had done it. We had raised a batch of chickens, transported them to the butcher's, and tomorrow Melissa would return to pick them up. Except for the few moments when they'd been crated and re-crated, the chickens lived a calm life on our farm, a life free of chemicals, a life of sunshine and wind and bugs and grass.

The alternative was living cramped in cages stacked five high in a long building, never to see the sun or eat an insect or fresh grass.

At one point on the drive home Melissa reached over and took my hand. "You know, because we've done this tonight, our friends and family will have safe, good-tasting chickens to put in their freezers."

I squeezed her hand. "I know. I just didn't think it would be so hard."

"Me neither," she replied.

I guess that was something all the authors I'd read had forgotten to mention in their books about raising animals. It would have been nice if at least one of them could have said, "Oh, yeah, and the first time you take animals to market so someone else can kill them, it sort of hurts."

oops

melissa loved her old tractor. It was a huge red Farmall 706, complete with hydraulics and a battered front loader. The tractor, its huge tires bulging above my head, was a mountain I had no interest in scaling. The forty-year-old behemoth was called a row crop tractor because it sets the farmer up high so she can see down the planted rows of the field. While the big red beast was Melissa's friend, I drew a line, and that tractor and I were on opposite sides.

While the tractor itself terrified me, the endless list of what one could hitch to the back of it intrigued me. Farmers had implements for every purpose: plow, drag, disc, no-till drill, bale fork, subsoiler, mower. Our tractor had an old-fashioned two-point hitch, which meant an implement attached to the tractor with, not surprisingly, two points. Trying to fit the two iron prongs of a plow into these two small iron openings rarely went smoothly. It was like plugging an electric cord into an outlet, only both the cord and outlet were a hundred times heavier.

We started by grunting and groaning and cussing, until I finally convinced Melissa that two women were no match for tractor implements that refused to fit together. That's when I drove to

Fleet Farm, a sort of Macy's for farmers, and bought Henry, a twenty-pound sledgehammer. Anything fit together if I whaled on it long enough with Henry. Of course the implement got banged up a bit, and my arms shook with weakness for hours afterwards, but Henry proved to be a very competent farmhand.

One late summer day, Melissa spent several blissful hours driving her beloved tractor over the north pasture, spreading five-hundred-dollars worth of grass and clover with her tractor and a rented seeder. The day went well. But the next day the tractor no longer worked. This was really bad news because rain was forecast for that afternoon, and with our sloping land, rain would wash our five hundred dollars right down into the creek. She needed to pull the neighbor's drag over the twenty-acre field to incorporate the seed.

Melissa removed the tractor's battery and took it to be tested at Larson's Implement, the tractor dealership in town. It was fine. She reattached the battery, then she tightened the solenoid and cracked it. Back into town for new solenoid. She installed the new solenoid with a gentler twist of the wrist, then turned the ignition key. Not even a dry grinding of gears. The old tractor still wouldn't start.

A kind soul at the implement dealer came out to the farm to see if he could help, and in just a few minutes he determined that the engine wouldn't run because of something Melissa had forgotten to do. Something really big and important. Like check the oil level. No oil, engine seizes up. Big mess. Melissa had been so busy and distracted that she'd forgotten.

Embarrassed and grief-stricken, she watched as Larson's massive tow truck winched our tractor up onto its metal grid trailer, and drove away. It would cost nearly as much to fix the tractor as it had cost to buy it. My head started to hurt.

Melissa swallowed a huge lump of pride and asked our neighbor Lyle if we could borrow not only his drag, but his tractor as well. The forecasted torrential downpour was only hours away.

I went back to cleaning the house for a friend's visit while Melissa headed for the field with the tractor and borrowed drag. A drag was a simple implement, nothing more than a grid of short iron teeth connected to a sixteen-foot pole, which was attached to the tractor with a chain. The teeth drag through the ground, roughing it up, combing the seed into the ground, sort of like a huge hairbrush with nasty bristles. Thirty minutes later Melissa reappeared. "I need your help."

"What happened?"

She sighed, and motioned to the pickup. "C'mon, I'll show you."

She drove me up onto the field and I could not speak. Twice around the field, and the tractor had suddenly stopped. Melissa turned around and found the entire drag had crawled up behind her and wrapped itself around the rear tire. A four-inch iron spike was now less than an inch away from puncturing the neighbor's tractor tire, which cost about eight hundred dollars apiece. One end of the drag's leading pole was buried deep in the ground. The whole mess was held captive by the chain pulled tight under the tire. There was no way to move the tractor. There was no apparent way to free the drag.

As I stared at the tangled mess that was once a drag, the real dangers of farming hit me for the first time. If an artist screwed up, she painted over her mistakes and started over. If an accountant screwed up, she cleared her calculator and started again. If a farmer screwed up, she could be dead. If the drag's chain hadn't caught on the tire, the drag would have crawled right over the driver's seat and Melissa would have been shish kebab.

This catastrophe occurred on the hill by the highway, where surely the occupants of every car whizzing by were pointing and laughing at our predicament. That gray pickup was probably a farmer from Wanamingo shaking his head at the two women "farmers." That red Buick was likely filled with businessmen on their way to Rochester, relieved to be wearing pinstriped suits rather than my striped OshKosh B'Gosh overalls.

Horrified, I returned to the shed and retrieved Henry. Back on the hill I faced the drag/tractor mess, feeling the eyes of dozens of scornful travelers burning into my back as they sped by. "Everyone is watching us," I wailed.

"I don't care," Melissa snapped. We whacked and pushed and pulled and dug.

My arms trembled, my back ached, and the drag was still buried tight against the tractor. My fear for Melissa came out sideways in anger as we struggled with the drag. Neither of us said out loud what might have happened to her if the drag hadn't jammed itself before reaching her. "How could you do this?" slipped from my lips.

Melissa's response was creative but unprintable. I shouted back, and we didn't stop yelling until fifteen minutes later, when, thanks to Henry and our four-wheel drive pickup pulling on the chain, we freed the drag without puncturing the tire. But what remained was not a pretty sight. Lyle's once-straight drag had reshaped itself into a boomerang. Any forward motion buried the ends of the bent iron rod right into the ground.

Exhausted, we watched the traffic in silence for a moment. Not one person looked our way, all too intent on their conversations or books or naps or cell phones to even notice the land they traversed. I was grateful for their apathy.

We dismantled the drag, stacked the pieces as best we could, and attached them to the tractor. Melissa drove back to Lyle's farm. "That's okay," Lyle said as he performed the classic one-handed farmer move: grab bill of cap, slide cap back, scratch top of head with same hand, replace cap. His voice was soft but he looked a little green; we realized later this wasn't because of the damage to the drag, but because he knew exactly what had almost happened to Melissa.

"That old drag's a piece of junk anyway," his twelve-year old son said. Nice try, kid, but Melissa still felt awful. After offering about two hundred times to pay for the damage, we thanked Lyle for the use of tractor and drag, then walked home.

Like a patch of crabgrass, Melissa wouldn't let go, insisting she drag the field before the rain came. Clouds thickened and roiled to the west. Time was running out. Melissa called another neighbor, and soon found herself atop Walter's little 8N Ford tractor, the one without any shocks under the worn metal seat.

"Be careful," I said.

Melissa took off her white Goodhue Elevator cap, ran her fingers, now stained with tractor grease and our dark clay soil, through her hair, then jammed the cap back onto her head. "Always."

Walter's drag was only about four feet wide, which meant Melissa's job would be like raking your lawn with a toothbrush. She bounced back and forth across that field for three hours. But she finished. She returned Walter's tractor and drag without so much as a scratch. The rain came—three days later.

That night we lay in bed, staring at the ceiling. Melissa was still so horrified she could barely speak. Exhaustion lined the pale skin around her eyes, and I could feel the tears gathering inside her. "How long before you can laugh about this?" I asked, still stinging from my grape disaster.

"Never, ever, ever," she replied in a shuddery voice.

"Hey, I know," I said. "Let's blame our parents."

"What?"

"They never taught us anything about tractors." Kids growing up on a farm learned things so early they weren't even aware the rest of the world didn't know them. They learned how to milk a cow, butcher a chicken, drive a tractor, bale hay, repair barbed wire fences, and be a midwife. Without that basic knowledge, people who wanted to farm were doomed to make mistakes. Some mistakes were irritating. Some were damned embarrassing. Some were expensive. Some were life threatening. We had managed to hit all of these in one day.

"But my parents aren't farmers. Neither are yours."

"So what? It's still their fault." I didn't stop until a weak smile finally flickered across her face. She would be fine.

finding our way in the dark

despite a new tractor engine, and a *few* upside-down grapevines, we *were* moving ahead. With my dad's help, we put in a haymow floor in the smaller barn. We kept building the inside fencing, but had a long way to go. We had fifty sheep. We had goats. We had chickens in our freezer. I had a job teaching writing, an editor who wanted to see more of my work, and no idea what to write about. Melissa and I daily struggled to find a way to work together, live together, and still enjoy each other's company.

Once, long before we'd started farming, Melissa had turned to me during a serious discussion and said, "You're my ocean liner."

"I beg your pardon?" I'd gained a few pounds that year, but didn't think she'd noticed.

She smiled ruefully, a little embarrassed, then continued. "I think you're emotionally a lot stronger than I am, so sometimes I think of you as this steady, stable ocean liner, and I'm this happy little dinghy tied on behind, happy and carefree, bouncing around in the waves."

"You're kidding."

"No."

"But I thought our relationship was more equal than that."

"Oh, it is." We shared responsibilities based on who did what the best. Melissa hated to cook slightly more than I did, so I cooked. I hated to clean the kitchen, so she would clean up. I could hammer a nail more accurately, was built for heavy lifting, and she had the patience to sew my coat buttons back on. "I know we rely on each other equally, but it's just this image I have."

I suppose I snorted, then changed the subject, half-confused and half-flattered. I think, however, that when one person in a relationship has a chronic health condition, like her headaches, there is a need on the other person's part to do more caretaking. I refused to do her work for her, so I didn't let her headaches intrude that way, but I think I might have absorbed that charming image of the ocean liner and the happy dinghy a little too completely.

Her pain was worse when she spent too much time on the tractor, but because I was not about to climb up on that massive, chugging beast, she did what needed to be done. But those tasks I could do to save her from pain, I did. I was the one to use the post pounder because the lift-and-slam motion gave her a nasty headache the next day. The post pounder was a heavy iron tube, closed off at one end and packed with enough iron to weigh over forty pounds. I slid the end onto the metal fence post, straightened the post, then began a lift-and-slam motion, pounding the post into the ground, always wearing ear protectors against the harsh clank of metal against metal.

One afternoon, instead of helping her headache, I made it ten times worse. Suffering from a headache but not wanting to miss anything, Melissa came into the barn while I was pounding a post. Once the post was in, the only way to get the heavy pounder off the post was to give a huge heave upward, practically flinging the cylinder over your right shoulder and letting it drop to the ground. Standing behind my right shoulder, she realized the post was almost in, and knew I'd be heaving the heavy iron pounder straight toward her. Unfortunately, before she moved, she looked up and became so enchanted with the view from the barn, the green valley sloping to the south, the bluebirds resting on small bushes, that she forgot to step back. The first I knew she was there was when I grunted, then heaved the post pounder up over my right shoulder, and directly onto her head. After a dozen ice packs and a few days' rest, she was fine.

A farm is a business, and must be run as such. We were both equal partners, and even though this was Melissa's dream, I was involved in every decision, almost every activity. Most of the time this worked well, but Melissa's anger and frustration had started to rise so gradually neither of us noticed, and we began to bash heads as repeatedly as Lancelot and Merlin did, only they were just horsing around and having fun. Melissa wanted to solve every problem her way. My way was usually to step back, think about it, puzzle it out, perhaps ask someone for help, sleep on it, then tackle it in the morning. No point doing something today if you can put it off until tomorrow.

Melissa's way was to sink her teeth into the problem and not let go until it was dark outside or cold, or she'd hurt herself, or broken something, or actually solved the problem. Only then could she move on to another problem.

Not only were we working out how to work together, but I was trying to find some balance between my inside life and my outside life. I'd begun to see that while there were great advantages to teaching via correspondence—never having to dress up or worry about bad hair days or having students call at all hours of the day or night—there were also distinct disadvantages. I lived at home. I worked at home as an instructor. I worked at home as a writer. I worked at home as a farmer. There was no getting away from any of it. If I needed a break from teaching or writing, I'd step outside, where I'd be confronted with Melissa needing help, or a sheep bleating, or two chickens fighting, or a fence that needed building, so I'd flee back inside the house.

The only safe place to go, where nothing was required of me, was the refrigerator, or the public library, or my mom's house. But since she lived two hours away, it just wasn't practical to show up on her doorstep, although some days I wanted nothing more than to collapse on my mom's sofa and beg her to take care of me. I doubt she would have said "I told you so," but I didn't dare risk it.

chicken sex

melissa enjoyed raising the broiler chickens so much
that she wanted chickens all year long. Laying hens
would give us fresh eggs every day. We could hatch some of the
eggs and make more chickens. What a deal. Farmers were always
trying to get rid of chickens, so she had no trouble buying twenty
hens of various sizes and colors: Silver-laced Wyandotte, Buff
Orpington, Rhode Island Red, Black Australorp, Speckled Sussex.

A hen can lay an egg just fine without a rooster, but if you want
the egg to hatch into a chick, you need a rooster. Melissa bought
one and we sat back to watch.

But instead of perching proudly on the "bleachers" Melissa had
built, this rooster, white with a smoky green tail and flamboyant
red comb, snuggled down into the nest box where the hens laid
their eggs. Great. A "cross-nester." We named him Serge, pronounced with a soft *g*. While we supported and encouraged
diversity, no chicken sex meant no fertilized egg, no chick.

Then Romeo appeared on the scene, peacock green and
proud. We rescued him from our friend's farm, where the other
roosters kicked him out the barn door every night. Winter would
have meant frozen death for poor Romeo.

Okay. Two roosters, twenty hens. Surely chicken sex would happen now.

It did. Even Serge found it within himself to do the deed. Soon broody hens sat on clutches of fertilized eggs. After three weeks, the eggs cracked and wet ugly bundles emerged. The chicks dried into cuteness, and slept under Mama's wings every night.

Good Serge. Good Romeo. But one day as the chickens roamed the yard, I noticed the boys had different styles. Serge brought flowers, lit golden tapers, poured goblets of champagne. There was a quiet mounting, brief fluttering of wings. Thank you, ma'am. Much obliged. May I call on you again?

Romeo, on the other hand, hid, waiting. Then, screaming, he chased the hen around the barn. Come back here, you stupid bitch. He grabbed the back of her head with his beak, flung her down, jumped her bones while she shrieked in distress. Wham. Bam. Feathers flew. He let her go, shook out his fine self. It was consensual, babe. Besides, you were asking for it.

"I don't like chicken sex," I said to Melissa as I chopped up carrots and celery. "I mean, I get the whole reproductive thing. But it can be so . . ."

"Violent. I know," she said as she sprinkled rosemary and oregano into the pot.

Then we ate Romeo.

Well, actually we didn't. But we *wanted* to. Melissa wasn't yet ready to kill a chicken, so we gave him to the elderly neighbors, and they ate him.

at long last, sheep sex

fall came and our pastures stopped growing, but we'd done our homework, so knew it was time to buy hay. Hay could be anything—alfalfa, grass, clover—anything green that was cut and baled. I continually confused the words *straw* and *hay,* until Melissa hammered it into my head that hay was food—it was green and contained nutrition. Straw was bedding—it was yellow and contained no food value because it was just the stalks left after a crop had been harvested. I smugly began to notice how many people erroneously talked about spreading hay for bedding. With the infinite patience of an experienced country woman, I would wearily point out their silly mistake.

Melissa ordered thirty large round bales and the farmer delivered them. Because our tractor wasn't dependable in the winter, and could get stuck easily, we set up the winter's supply of food all at once. Melissa happily fired up the tractor and moved the bales into seven rows of four bales, the bales spread about ten feet apart. We put up Electronet so the sheep could only get to four bales at a time. When it was all done, we stood back and laughed. The green mounds, arranged so carefully, so precisely, reminded us both of a mysterious circle of stones. We had created Hayhenge.

We also purchased a used grain bin and filled it full of corn for the sheep. While they didn't necessarily need grain, we wanted to give them some extra energy as we moved toward the breeding season. We started the sheep very slowly on corn, at first offering just a little so their rumens could handle it.

A ruminating animal has four stomachs, the rumen, reticulum, omasum, and abomasum. Food hits the rumen first, which functions like a huge fermentation vat where microorganisms begin breaking everything down. The animal regurgitates the food, bringing it up for a little happy cud chewing, then swallows it, then brings it back up for more masticating if needed. If humans ruminated, we could enjoy a pepperoni pizza with olives not just once, but two or three times.

Once it's been chewed enough, then the food moves on to the other three stomachs. It's a complex system, and if the rumen lacks the correct bacteria, it won't work right. If a new food is introduced too quickly, the rumen hasn't had time to develop the bacteria necessary to break that food down, so it bloats up like a balloon, and the animal could die.

The sheep came to adore the corn, and raced for the feeders every morning. I did a few school visits to make money and promote my books.

In our small town, word got around that I was a published author. Women's groups asked me to come speak. Schools asked me to come speak. The newspaper ran an article on me. But it had been two years since my two picture books had come out. As for the third manuscript, I'd revised and revised, but still my editor wasn't satisfied. The story just wasn't working. Finally we both gave up and let the story die quietly. He nearly bought two more manuscripts, but internal company problems interfered with both, so he was unable to give me contracts for either.

Everywhere I went in town, I heard some version of this question: When is your next book coming out? I didn't know how to answer that, and I felt too embarrassed to think clearly. It seemed petty to launch into a detailed explanation about how hard it really was to sell a manuscript for publication, how publishers received up to ten thousand manuscripts a year for only fifty or so publishing slots. It wasn't really fair to ask when my next book was out, for that implied it was under my control. It wasn't. Later they began asking if I had another book coming out. I didn't have an answer for that one either. I was trying, I really was, but until I sold another manuscript, I had no way to answer the questions. Besides, I was just going through a temporary slump. When people found out I farmed, they'd nod knowingly. "Oh, I'm sure that gives you lots to write about." Cripes. Absolutely not. But what was wrong with me? A tiny worry washed over me—maybe I really wasn't a writer.

But I was a shepherd—sort of. September, October, November passed, and December arrived. The ram lambs and their sperm stayed safely behind the electric fence, just as I'd planned. No unauthorized sheep sex. But they would if they could have. The ewe lambs began cycling, bleating suggestively through the fence. The ram lambs paced, pushing against the red metal gate, the only thing not electrified, until their wool was pink. They bashed heads in frustration, mounting each other without gratification. The rams were still lambs, but somehow their necks had disappeared into thick massive shoulders over the summer. Their noses had broadened, their chests filled out, their bleats deepened.

December 17 dawned cold and gray. Today was the day. I put a big red star on the calendar and wanted to call all our friends. After months of planning and waiting, today our animals would breed. They were going to make baby sheep. Amazing.

First, we had to strap nylon marking harnesses onto the ram lambs. Once we strapped the harnesses across each ram's brisket or chest, we'd attach a three-inch by four-inch marking crayon, about one inch thick. We chose blue and orange from the rainbow of choices in the sheep supply catalog. Theory was that as a ram mounted a ewe, he'd leave a waxy mark on her rump so we'd know she'd been bred. If we had a reluctant ram, we needed to know about it. We would put the blue chalk on Rudy, the orange on Otis.

We entered the ram pen, which started my heart pounding to be so near these wild guys, even though we were both armed with shepherd's crooks for either catching them around the neck or bashing them on the noses if they got too rowdy. But neither Rudy nor Otis wanted to have anything to do with us. We wanted to catch Otis first, the friendlier of the two, but ended up slamming ourselves to the ground repeatedly until we learned to work together, and finally pinned him to the ground. While I struggled to maintain my grip on him, Melissa started putting on the harness. "Wait, that's not right," she muttered. Some straps went over his back, others around his legs and across his chest. She tried several times, but none of the clasps fit right.

By now my arms were trembling and my knees were on fire from grinding into the gravel floor. "I can't—" Otis yanked himself free and I fell on my hands and knees.

"Perfect," Melissa said, and she used me as model to figure out which strap went where.

"This is interesting," I said as yet another boundary came crashing down around my ears, this bizarre apparatus draped over me.

"Stop moving. There, that's the way it goes." We finally got the harnesses strapped onto the rams, the crayons attached to the harnesses.

Relieved we didn't get hurt, we separated the rams, then separated the ewe lambs into two groups, one for each ram. Pheromones flew across fences. The rams bellowed, the ewes answered. The waiting was over. Everyone was ready for reproductive sex. Let's make some lambs.

Female sheep cycle every seventeen days or so. This means that, unlike humans, they aren't ready to experience intimacy at the drop of a hat. If the ewe isn't within a day or two of her "time," she won't have a thing to do with the ram. And if she won't stand still, he can't rub his nice new chalk marker all over her rump.

Melissa opened the small gate and let Otis into the pen with his flock. Glad to have a new place to explore, Otis didn't understand the change in his fortune as he ambled toward the group of twenty-five ewe lambs. But when he got close enough to smell them, the poor ram lamb suddenly got it. He ran into the ewes, scattering them, then totally lost focus. He ran from ewe to ewe, sniffing her nether regions, curling his lip seductively, then running to the next. The ewes each moved away, continuing to clean up spilled corn off the ground.

Finally Otis set his sights on a sweet ewe lamb with a heart-shaped face.

"Here we go," I said, trying to ignore the freezing temperature and lack of sun.

Otis nuzzled her ear, lip curled. She walked away. He followed, nuzzling her flank. She walked away. He followed, nuzzling more insistently. She trotted away. He followed. She ran, cutting a large figure eight through two inches of snow. He followed. Every time she stopped, he touched her and she started running again. They ran the same figure-eight pattern for twenty minutes. Poor Otis had chosen a young lady who wasn't at day seventeen in her cycle.

I stomped my cold-deadened feet and rubbed my mittens together. "We'll never have lambs born on this place," I said.

"Wait," Melissa said. "There he goes." Otis threw one front leg around the ewe's hip, but she ran and he slipped off. We let Rudy in with his flock and he ignored the ladies entirely, immediately dashing to the feeder looking for corn.

We watched for another twenty minutes as Otis ran his figure-eight and Rudy did nothing. Finally we stumbled back to the house to soothe our disappointment with double-strength hot chocolate. Talk about anticlimactic.

The next morning, miracle of miracles, four of Rudy's ewes had blue butts. Sheep sex had happened. Nothing on Otis's side. My sister and brother-in-law bravely left the warmth of Florida to spend a few days at Christmas with us. Sandy and Rick gamely bundled up every morning and went up to the barn with us to help count marked butts. They called out the numbers as Melissa wrote them in her notebook. New blue butts appeared every day in Rudy's pen. Nothing on Otis's side.

"Maybe he has pizzle rot. Or not enough motility, whatever the hell that is." I'd clearly been reading too many sheep books. "Or maybe he needs more corn," I said. "He's getting too tired chasing them to actually finish things." Just then a ewe lamb walked by Melissa. The sunlight, just right, revealed the faintest shimmer of peach on her rump (the ewe's, that is.) We looked closer. Half of the ewes had faint peach rumps. Otis had been doing his job; it was the crayon that had failed to perform.

Melissa and I hugged. "Babies," she whispered. "In five months, we're going to have baby lambs everywhere."

Her joy flamed my own. Yes. We were doing this. We were shepherds. We were farming. Something almost like anxiety cramped my guts, but I decided it was just something I'd eaten. Besides, it was too late to turn back now.

hit by a farm

what could possibly go wrong?

Luckily, of all the areas our sheep books addressed, the one they each covered with great relish and exquisite detail was lambing. Some provided handy drawings of the process. One author had the poor taste to include photos of an actual lamb being born. At least the photos were in black and white.

When Melissa and I had taken that first weekend class on raising sheep, Janet had showed the class a video on lambing. I spent most of that hour either studying the ceiling or the woodgrain of the desk in front of me, so I remembered little. As May approached, however, I did recall one section of the video where the vet used a floppy stuffed lamb to show the proper presentation for birth. Standing in for the ewe was a clear bassinet with a hole cut out of one end. The vet tipped the bassinet slightly to show the angle of the womb, tucked the stuffed toy into the bassinet, its nose and feet pointing straight toward that hole. Smiling encouragingly the whole time, the vet gently worked the lamb toward the hole, then pulled the front feet and nose out the hole. Of course the rest of the body followed. "This is how most of your lambs will be born," he said with a smile I suddenly realized was forced. Clearly, he was lying.

That winter Melissa and I started studying the books. As she pored over the diagrams, her eyes lit up at all the possibilities, and at the idea that she'd be able to get involved in the birthing process. I could barely sleep some nights. Shepherds measured success by lambing percentage rates, and by lambing survival rates. A 200 percent crop meant that two lambs survived for every ewe. A 100 percent survival rate was one lamb per ewe. We had no idea what we were doing, so every lamb born would surely die, giving us a lambing percentage of 0 percent.

The books were so matter-of-fact it made me crazy, as if dealing with birthing problems were a perfectly natural part of life. Certainly not my life. My favorite was the advice for a lamb born with breathing problems: "grasp it firmly by the hind legs and swing it aggressively in an arc several times in order that centrifugal force will expel the mucus. Make sure you have a good grip on the lamb to avoid throwing it out of the barn." Wow.

But I was getting ahead of myself. First the lamb had to actually come out. A normal birth was both front feet first with the nose resting on the hooves. Anything other than this might cause difficulties for the ewe and require our intervention. The description of possible abnormal births went on for pages. They seemed to fall into eight categories.

(1) Large head or shoulders, which makes for a tight delivery. Pull gently from side to side. Pull what from side to side? Use mineral oil to lubricate lamb. Ouch. How does one get the mineral oil around the lamb? If the lamb's stuck, there isn't room for anything else, right?

(2) Front half of lamb out, hips locked. Whose hips? The lamb's? The ewe's? Mine? The video vet assured us if the legs and head came out, the rest would follow. I decided the book, with its alarmist talk of lambs not coming out, was lying, and that I would now place my trust in that nice vet and his stuffed lamb.

(3) Head and one leg out, with one leg turned back. The leg

that is folded back may hang up on the ewe's pelvic bone, so the lamb can't get out. Reach in, gently lift the leg, push the lamb back, straighten the leg and bring over the pelvic bone. Fine. No problem. Will the ewe stand there quietly while one of us "reaches" in? If the head and one leg are already in the birth canal, how will there be room for a human hand and arm? Does the author think we have *eyes* on our fingertips? How will we know we have a leg, the right leg, or the pelvic bone?

(4) Head out, with both legs turned back, or both legs out, with head turned back. This is one of the most difficult because you cannot just pull on the legs and expect the head to follow; it's twisted back and will only move farther back if you pull. Instead, gently push the front legs back into the birth canal and under the lamb's body. But here's where they lost me. If the ewe has already ejected half the lamb, is she going to relax and let us put it back in? If a woman gave birth and the doctor said, "Sorry, ma'am, but we have to put this baby back inside you for a minute," how cooperative would *that* female be? The other option was to find the head, once again with those eyes on your fingertips, then pull it forward by holding the lower jaw between thumb and forefinger. When the lamb's head is facing the right direction, find the front legs and pull head and legs out. I loved all this talk of "find." If there were four legs, how the hell did you know which was a front leg and which was a back leg?

(5) Hind feet coming first. You might have to pull the lamb to help it out. But make sure you have two hind feet, not one hind foot and one front foot. Oh, shit.

(6) Breech. The lamb is trying to come out butt-first, which doesn't work. You must reach in, "find" the back legs, bend them gently back then pull the lamb out with these legs.

(7) Lamb lying crossways. I couldn't even bear to read this section.

And finally, (8) All four legs presented at once. Man, oh, man, this just couldn't happen with our animals. Ours would have the "stuffed lamb" birth, lined up beautifully in that tipped bassinet, coming out all fluffy and clean.

Multiple births presented their own particular problems. If twins, mixed up, tried coming out at once, there would be too many feet in the birth canal, and the rest of the lamb couldn't exit. Sort out which foot belongs where. Is it the right front of Lamb One or the back left of Lamb Two? Tie strings on the two front legs of the same lamb and feel back to the body to make sure they both, in fact, belong to the same body before you start pulling. Push one lamb back to make room for the delivery of the first one. The more I read these directions, the more it seemed the vagina and uterus of a sheep were roomy areas with plenty of space to put both hands in, count lamb legs, tie colored yarn onto each leg, perhaps knit a sweater or two.

Twins may present as one coming backward, one forward. In this case, pull out the reversed lamb first. Sometimes the head of one twin is presented between the forelegs of the other twin, a confusing situation, but rare, said the book. I strained to read between the lines. Surely it said "this only happens to very experienced shepherds. Ewes would never try this on a totally green shepherd."

During any of these abnormal presentations, a lamb could die inside the ewe—lack of oxygen during the birth process. Most of the time the ewe's body would go ahead and give birth anyway. But you might have to reach in and pull out the dead lamb. If the dead lamb was so large it couldn't be pulled out, a veterinarian would have to dismember the lamb to remove it.

I felt faint.

Lambing loomed ahead of me like a giant black hole, one of those swirling phenomenon that clutches your spaceship in its gravitational pull and sucks you in, even as you're frantically flipping all your levers and pushing all your buttons and sending out a mayday call. There was no way around lambing; all I could do was go through it.

dancing with goats in the moonlight

that winter cabin fever really hit as I read and worried about all those babies coming in the spring. Lancelot and Merlin the goats also got cabin fever as they spent the cold months living in Camelot, our name for the domed white calf hutch warmed by composting goat manure, straw, and the goats' body heat. During really cold spells they never left their round home so we provided room service, bringing them hay so they wouldn't have to walk outside.

Now and then Lance would kick Merlin out of Camelot. I'd look out the dining-room window and see poor Merlin standing outside the thin, braided rug that served as the hutch's door, his brown hair puffed up against the cold. One of us would pull on our winter gear, stomp down the hill, yank Lance out and shove Merlin back in. By the time we'd returned to the house and stripped off coat, boots, and mittens, Lance had kicked Merlin out again. Luckily they'd made up by dusk, so Merlin could get back inside before the temperature plummeted even farther.

We were so relieved when the cold spell snapped and the temperature rose above zero. One balmy night, probably five degrees above zero, the moon rose full and white in the east. I noticed the goats were outside, enjoying the warmer weather. "Let's go play with them," Melissa said. So we bundled up in coats, earmuffs, boots, and mittens, and slid down the icy hill to the goat pen. The goats nickered with delight and ran to the gate. Everything shimmered blue under the moon, bright enough I could have read a book.

Goats are gregarious, playful creatures, and soon we were chasing each other around the pen, our white breath puffing like icy dragon's fire. I'd lope from one side to the other, Merlin and Lance at my heels, leaping and twisting and kicking the air. Then nickering, they'd run back to Melissa. She'd hide behind the hutch and when Merlin found her, he'd rear up with pleasure, whirl, and race around the pen. Their hooves clicked on the icy patches, and our boots crunched as we broke through crusty snow. A great horned owl called from the woods in the valley below.

The goats shone blue-white in the moonlight and we laughed and played with them until we had to open our coats and pull off gloves. I reached down to hug Lance; he leaned quietly against me for a moment, snorted, then whirled around to lure me back into the dance.

time to take it off
(the wool, that is)

march arrived with blistering winds one day, and moist, clammy air the next. The snow melted, froze, melted again. A thick skin of frozen snow covered everything.

Drew called us the day before shearing. "You gals get them ewes into the barn tonight. I don't want to be shearing wet wool." Yes, sir! Drew was a friend from our SEMPSA group, and sported a thick black beard and an even thicker southern Illinois accent. We put the sheep in the barn, one of the few nights they'd been in there all winter. Because they walked around with five inches of wool, they didn't need shelter, carrying their "barns" on their backs. When the wool came off, of course, they'd have access to the barn twenty-four hours a day.

Why shear? Giving birth would be more sanitary without all that wool to catch blood and feces; less wool would help the new-born lambs find the teats more easily. Life in the summer would be easier for the sheep with shorter wool. The market for wool was so poor, however, that selling the wool would barely pay for the cost of having it removed.

On shearing day the sun was out, but the temperature was only twenty degrees. Drew arrived in his blue pickup and we helped him set up. First came a sheet of plywood covered with indoor-outdoor carpeting, then the battered metal box that held his shears. We strung an extension cord from the nearest outlet to his shearing spot, then set up the wobbly metal frame for the seven-foot plastic wool bag, and helped Drew attach the first bag.

We'd assembled a devoted team of family and friends. My mom brought chocolate cake, chili, and cream of broccoli soup. Melissa's mom brought pop and hot cider. We started up the space heater in the feed room so when people weren't helping or watching, they could huddle around the heat.

The first job was to catch a sheep and lead her over to the shearing area. Melissa grabbed the first ewe lamb, but the ewe leapt away. Finally it took both Melissa and Mary to catch the ewe and practically carry her over to Drew, who grabbed her and expertly flipped her onto her rump, pulling her back so she rested against his thighs.

The buzz of electric shears drowned out most of our voices. Drew bent over at the waist, letting his upper body fall nearly over the sheep so his back muscles didn't have to hold him up, the recipe for total exhaustion in fifteen minutes. Drew slid the noisy shears over the ewe's chest and down her belly, slipping neatly but quickly around the teats, then around the anus. A few strokes down each thigh and the legs were clear. The wool hung together, a cloudy cloak falling off the sheep's back. Then came the scary cut, when he brought the shears up one side and across the ewe's throat, the shears buried in so much wool Drew's only guide was his experience. Ten more strokes and the entire fleece fell away in a billowing mass of pale yellow. Drew let the ewe go then moved away. I rushed in and gathered the fleece in my arms, but it was like trying to pick up water. Somehow I got the fleece from the ground and into the bag.

Melissa caught another ewe. "Hey, don't drag that sheep on its butt," Drew yelled at Melissa. "You're getting the wool full of crap."

The ewe kicked free and fled back into the pack. Melissa caught it again, but it slipped from her grasp. By now Drew was standing idle, waiting impatiently for something to shear. "You gonna catch that sheep or just play with it?" he growled, winking at his audience as Melissa wrestled with the sheep.

When ten fleeces had gone in the bag, Drew looked at me, cheek bulging with a plug of tobacco. "'Bout time you climb on up inside that bag. I want it packed tight, you hear? We gotta get twenty-five fleece in there."

Someone steadied the wobbly frame as I climbed up its ladder. I lowered one leg inside the bag, then perched on the edge, gazing over the scene below me, steadying myself against one of the roof beams. I was a little fearful, actually, given my strong claustrophobia, so I hesitated and surveyed the scene. Drew bent over the next sheep, and Melissa knelt in front of him, fascinated. "Get any closer and this damn sheep's gonna kick your teeth out." Melissa reluctantly stepped back, but I knew it was only a matter of time before she asked to try this herself. Mary and another friend caught the next ewe. Melissa's sister Peg waited for the next fleece.

My stepfather leaned against the broom, favoring his bad knee. My mom and Melissa's mom stood outside the pen, gloved hands wrapped around steaming cups of coffee. I waved dramatically, shouting above the buzzing shears. "Bye, Mom. Bye, everyone!" My appreciative crowd whooped as I slid off the frame and disappeared into the bag. My mom spent her childhood in a wool bag. Her dad would throw her in, and she couldn't climb out until the bag was full.

The bag was warm, and while I could see shapes and colors through the cloudy plastic, I was in my own little world, except for the square of barn roof visible above me. "Coming with a fleece, Cath," Peg said, and I reached up, mouth and eyes closed, as eight pounds of wool fell around my head and shoulders. I pulled it down to my feet, and began stomping it down around the outside edges of the bag. My claustrophobia didn't kick in, so I knew I could make it. I stomped almost constantly between fleeces, determined not to disappoint Drew or embarrass myself.

Finally, after thirty minutes or so, I could just peek over the edge of the wool bag. Another few fleeces, and I could hang my arms over the edge. My legs were quivering from the constant stomping, but I was now standing high above the bag, my head in the rafters.

"How many?" Drew roared.

We counted the naked sheep now scampering around the nearby pen. "Twenty-five!" I shouted, and grinned at Drew's pleased nod. Ready to let someone stomp the next bag so I could rest, I climbed down and Drew taped the bag shut and set up another one.

My hands had been softened and my boots shined smooth by the wool's lanolin. Some people don't like the smell of unwashed wool, but I'd come to like it, and had decided that from this point on I would only wear wool for warmth. Now that I was a shepherd, no more polar fleeces would die on my behalf. Wool is a natural fiber, and just makes more sense. One of the friends helping us shear was a knitter, and knew a great deal about wool. It turns out that wool really is an amazing fiber. The lanolin repels water. Each wool fiber is made up of millions of coiled springs that stretch and give rather than break, making wool naturally elastic. These crimped fibers also form little pockets of air that act as insulators, keeping sheep, and humans, warm and dry. Wool can absorb up to 30 percent of its own weight before feeling wet; synthetic fibers can only absorb about 4 percent before feeling wet. All this information, plus the great satisfaction of two massive bags filled with our own wool, convinced me I wanted to keep some of the wool, spin it, dye it, and knit our own sweaters, scarves, and socks. Of course, I would do this in my vast amounts of spare time.

The day was long and hard, but satisfying. We had so many helpers we kept the board swept clean as Drew moved from one end to the other. The constant buzz of the shears stopped only when he oiled the blades or took a rare break. The rams, once a bit intimidating with their bulk, were now ridiculously tiny, and so angry at being shorn they bashed heads until they drew blood. Drew said they no longer recognized each other, so needed to let "the new guy" know who was boss. The shorn ewes looked goofy and incredibly young. But they scampered about more, obviously happy to be free of all that weight. Apparently a naked sheep was a happy sheep.

I was exhausted but strangely content. The day had tested me and I'd measured up. Now if I could perform as well during lambing, my transition to farmer would be as smooth and effortless as I'd hoped.

Ha.

in the bedroom

Some people are sure kinky things go on inside a lesbian couple's bedroom, so perhaps it's time to fling those bedroom doors wide open for public viewing.

One representative night had its origins in Melissa's desire to learn how to shear a sheep, fueled by our shearing day. Even when my mom told Melissa of my grandfather's back pain after shearing, Melissa still wanted to learn. So early spring she attended a two-day class through the University of Wisconsin, and I came along, anxious for us to have time together. My mom and stepfather watched the farm.

I spent my time sitting in the motel, trying to write, but actually reading novels and watching VH1. At noon the first day, Melissa returned to the hotel, her entire front from ankles to shoulders stained with manure and greasy with lanolin. She dropped back onto the bed with a groan, arms flung wide.

"How's it going?" I asked.

"God, I can't move," she moaned. I brought lunch in and she ate and drank lying down, then I helped her up and she drove back for more. She hung in there, ending the weekend just as excited about shearing as when we'd arrived. She bought a set of electric shears and was determined to keep practicing.

People with small flocks had trouble getting shearers, so Melissa's name quickly got around. A woman called and asked Melissa to shear her flock of ten.

The night before Melissa was to shear, I brushed my teeth while Melissa sat on the bed studying her shearing "cheat sheet." Experienced shearers had worked out the most efficient pattern of cuts, diagramed clearly on this sheet. What wasn't as obvious was the placement of the shearer's feet and knees. When set back on its rump, a sheep will go fairly limp as long as it feels supported. The shearer stands over the sheep, using feet, knees, and thighs to support the animal, shifting slightly to position the sheep for the next cut in the pattern.

Melissa bent over the paper, muttering, "I've forgotten what to do with my feet. Tomorrow's going to be a disaster."

I looked toward the bed, the covers pulled back to reveal fresh clean sheets, my pillow plumped, a new library book waiting on my bedside table. I sighed, then dropped to the floor.

"Okay, baby," I said. "Shear me."

She gave me a funny look, then her eyes brightened and she jumped up. "Perfect," she said. Cheat sheet in hand, she moved behind me, pressing her knees against my back. She studied the sheet, then grabbed my chin and tipped my head back. She cupped her hand around an imaginary clipper.

"Okay, cut down the chest like so." She tapped my knees and my legs dropped open. "Okay, cut along the crotch, then up inside left thigh, then inside right thigh."

"Oooh, baby," I swooned.

"Hush now. Okay, up the outside left hip, then shift." She moved her right foot and I slumped to the right, my cheek flattened against the inside of her knee. "Up the side, up the back."

She moved her foot again and I slid all the way to the floor, where I came face to face with a massive clump of dog hair under the bed. She checked her cheat sheet again.

"Okay, finish the back, then pull sheep up by the ear—" I shot back up on my own. She shifted her left foot, and we repeated the same steps until I was once again on the floor, curled around Melissa's other foot. "Finish down the back, and you're done." She stood upright, triumphant.

I stared at her slender ankle. "Was it good for you, babe?"

"Yeah, yeah, it was great. Sit up and we'll do it again." She tugged at my arm and I sat up.

"Wow," I said. "Multiple shearings."

We practiced over and over again. After another twenty minutes, Melissa finally felt ready. I staggered to my feet, brushed the dust off my robe, then collapsed on the bed, spent.

ready or not, here they come

a month before lambing, Melissa came clattering into the house.

"Time to trim hooves," Melissa said, eyebrows pulled together.

"We'd planned that for yesterday," I snapped. "I had time yesterday afternoon, but you didn't do it then."

"I couldn't. Someone had to fix the mower so you can mow the vineyard. Today I can trim hooves."

"But I was going to write. I have an idea for another story, and I need to do some research at the library."

"But their hooves are dangerously long. They could start going lame. I'm sorry, Cath, but we can't wait any longer. Can you write later?"

She was right. Those hooves did need trimming. These sheep were my animals too, and I loved them, so I slid into my overalls, already well perfumed with Eau de Manure, and helped give fifty reluctant sheep their pedicures.

When done, I barely had the energy to take off my filthy clothes before falling into a heap on the bed. My computer stayed quiet. Who wanted to read a story about trimming sheep hooves? Only someone interested in how wet manure can pack in tightly under the hoof edges, and how the green stuff must be scraped out and how pockets of pus sometimes form and must be drained. And if that doesn't turn your stomach, then you don't have one.

May came, and our sheep grew wider and wider and wider. The poor things grunted softly as they lay down, as they dragged their swollen bellies up to the water trough. They adopted a pensive, thoughtful look, or as pensive and thoughtful as sheep could look. I, on the other hand, just looked worried, that sort of sheep-cornered-by-a-wolf look, like I was about to get run over by a tractor but couldn't step out of the way.

As May 13, our due date, approached, I grilled Melissa each time she left the farm. "How long will you be gone? What if someone goes into labor?"

"One hour. I have to buy sheep mineral and corn."

"You'll go to the elevator and come right back?"

"Of course."

She was working at the Vet Clinic afternoons, but I was confident the first lamb wouldn't be born when I was alone. So on May 11, a bright sunny afternoon, I walked up to the barn to feed the ewes their corn. Tomorrow we would move them out onto pasture, where they would start giving birth to their lambs.

The sheep milled around the entrance to the barn, bleating and raising up dust as they waited for me. One sheep moved aside, and I found myself face to face with a perfectly formed, miniature sheep, a sheep who'd been shrunk a dozen times. It took my brain a minute to register. This was a baby. I stared stupidly at the newborn.

"Oh, my god," I breathed. I had never seen a newborn lamb. I had no idea how old it was. The unconcerned ewes paid it little attention. They could crush it! And colostrum! It needed colostrum. This was the first milk a mammal received, rich in nutrients for a good start on life. I checked my watch. Melissa wouldn't be home for two more hours. It could die by then. It had to nurse!

Ohmygodohmygodohmygod. Adrenalin pumped through my system. I was the lamb's only hope. I watched, horrified, as the lamb wove its way through the forest of hooves, then stood next to a ewe. That must be the mother. Somehow I got all the sheep out of the barn except the ewe and her lamb. Then I herded those two into a smaller pen. Still trembling, I reached for the lamb but it scampered away. I lunged again and again, finally snagging a back leg. Warm and surprisingly light, the lamb was a miracle. He had two huge ears sticking straight out from his head, two gray-brown eyes, one white nose, four dainty legs, and two tiny testicles. We'd made a baby boy.

With this fragile bundle cradled against my chest, I lunged for the bleating ewe, succeeding the second time in pushing her up against the barn wall. Warm wool filled my nostrils as I pressed the top of my head against the ewe. I put the lamb down under the teat. "Drink, little one," I said. "You need to drink."

But nothing happened. I pushed him closer, but still no sucking action of any kind. Melissa had told me about stripping the teat, pulling gently on it to express milk and clear the teat of obstruction. Feeling self-conscious as I took one of the ewe's warm teats in my hand, I did this, pleased when a white thread shot out onto the straw. She had milk, but the lamb wouldn't drink. Near panic, I finally looked closer at the lamb. He was clean, white and fluffy, totally dry. I felt his belly. Round and full, very full.

I sat back on my heels. What a dolt. The lamb was hours old—I know now probably seven or eight hours old, nearly a toddler. Both the ewe and lamb stared at me, the lamb wide-eyed at this two-legged monster who'd invaded his world, and the ewe, eyes scolding as she chewed her cud. I apologized, then laughing with relief, brought them hay and water.

When Melissa came home, I said nonchalantly, "Got something to show you." We ambled up to the barn, where she whooped in delight at the sight of the little white lamb. She caught him and inspected him just as I had done. He was beautiful, and had come without any difficulty, almost as if the stork had deposited the lamb on our farm.

the first bad day

the rest of the ewes picked a cold, blustery morning four days later to start giving birth. The first ewe picked the windiest spot in the paddock and started bleating in confusion. She circled a few times, pawed the ground, lay down, then out slid a wet, oddly shaped bundle, encased in mucous. It looked like a soggy, spindly, drowned animal. But when the ewe began cleaning off the newborn's face and nostrils—thank goodness her maternal instincts kicked in—the lamb, not dead at all, struggled to lift its wobbly head and take in this new bright, windy world.

Then the ewe bleated, lay down, and delivered another. Now she had two lambs to clean. After fifteen minutes the first lamb stood up on wobbly legs, the second lay shivering and wet, hypothermic. The lambs bleated. The mother bleated. The other sheep, all new at this, paced in alarm at all the bleating.

Then a second ewe gave birth. I stood in the nearby row of trees, hunched against the cutting spring wind. How long did it take a lamb to stand up? When should we intervene? Then a third ewe went into labor, but with her lamb out only a few inches, she started following the second ewe's lamb, trying to adopt or "granny" it. Wind howled through the narrow band of box elders.

We returned to the original set of twins. The first lamb was up and nursing, but the second lamb still wasn't up, so we brought him inside. We toweled him off, but now what? He needed colostrum, so we fed him a bottle. But he either didn't know how to swallow, or couldn't, so without knowing it, we filled his lungs with milk. He died. Melissa lay the body outside the back door, the day's reminder of our ineptitude.

We called our mentor Paul and he, bless his heart, came right over. By then we had another hypothermic lamb. Paul showed Melissa how to hold the lamb on her lap, how to slide the slim rubber feeding tube down the lamb's throat, then how to listen into the tube. Breathing meant the tube was in the lungs; bubbling sounds meant the tube was properly in the stomach. Then I poured in the colostrum I'd heated on the stove.

I hadn't expected we'd need to warm up cold lambs in May. Melissa brought in a heat lamp and we hung it over a box in the basement. Terrified baby cries drifted up the stairs while I stood in the kitchen and wrung my hands. What if the mothers didn't take their babies back? The memory of that easy first lamb, born on his own on a sunny day, faded. Wringing my hands wasn't terribly productive, but it was my own unique contribution. So much for the romance of farming.

ear tags and
little rubber bands

after that, the weather improved. Melissa and I went out every morning to see if anyone had been born during the night. Not much happened at night, but every few days we'd come across a ewe with a lamb born at night, now happily nursing. Because our ewes were first-time lambers, most would have singles, a normal situation for young animals. But next year we expected their genetics to kick in and all have twins.

Now and then we saw a ewe go into labor. She wandered off by herself, choosing the spot to give birth. She started walking in circles, bleating softly. She lay down, got up, lay down, got up, confused at the odd contractions pulsing through her.

After we watched for thirty minutes, Melissa stood. "I think we should catch her and see what's going on in there," she said, a gleam in her eye.

"But what if that rushes the birth? Why do we have to get involved so soon?"

Melissa thought a minute, then dropped back down onto her haunches. "Okay, we'll wait."

One minute later I couldn't stop myself. "Maybe it's been too long. If we wait, the lamb might die. Shouldn't we be helping?"

This helpful conversation took place about three times every day. I don't know why Melissa didn't appreciate my contribution.

Now and then a ewe had clearly been in labor too long, so we chased her around until we were all tired, caught her, then I held her down while Melissa tugged on her long plastic glove, and slipped her hand inside the ewe. Melissa muttered to herself as she blindly sorted out the tiny legs inside the ewe. She seemed to have those eyes on her fingertips, for she had quickly learned to sort out a lamb's parts inside the sheep. "There . . . that leg was bent back."

"How can you tell that?"

"It helps to close my eyes, then I can see with my hand."

As the days passed, more tiny white lambs scampered by their mothers' sides. Melissa recorded the new additions every day in a small notebook she took to the pasture. I transferred the information into our records in the house. She filled a big pink plastic carrier with all the goodies she needed to process each new lamb. Because our lambs were born out on pasture instead of in a barn, we couldn't corner the lambs in a pen. Once a lamb was twelve hours old, it was fast enough to outrun us, so we gave each newborn lamb a few hours to nurse, to get its bearings, then we snuck up and caught it.

Melissa gave each lamb a shot of vitamins, dipped the navel in iodine, attached a plastic numbered ear tag, felt for a full belly to make sure it had been nursing, then checked the sex. If it was a male, she pulled out a nasty-looking tool called a burdizo, a silver, clamplike thing. She found the slender cords running to the testicles, slid the burdizo jaws over these cords, then apologized. We'd both grimace as she squeezed the jaws together, crushing the cords so the testicles would eventually atrophy. I was too squeamish to do this, so it was Melissa's job.

After a few of these castrations, I mentioned the alternative. "What if we use the rubber band thing like Paul does? The band cuts off the blood, it's not painful after the first few seconds. The testicles atrophy and fall off."

Melissa nodded. The burdizo was tricky, and if she didn't get both cords, we might end up with intact, or fertile, rams. We soon switched to rubber bands.

If the ewe had twins, I held one squirming lamb while Melissa processed the other. During this whole procedure, the ewe was circling us, bleating angrily. The bleating was normal, and temporary. Seconds after they're born, lambs learn their mother's voice, and she theirs. That was how they sorted themselves out at night—lambs calling, and Mom responding until they heard one another over the din, and the lambs scampered to the ewe's side. Melissa enjoyed the bleating, using it to assess what the flock might be up to. For some reason, it triggered my adrenal system, and I found it as relaxing as having someone shout "Your house is on fire!" in my ear all day.

another bad day,
but who's counting?

in the midst of lambing, I still did school visits. I also volun-
teered as a tutor for an adult literacy program, meeting with
a Vietnamese woman once a week, helping her improve her halt-
ing English. I accepted a position on the library board, and
attended those meetings once a month. I even drove up to Minneapolis for my biweekly writing group with six other children's
writers. As I sat there, listening to my friends read their work, I
could not stop thinking about how much my life had changed.
Their lives were as full as mine, but mine had suddenly become
foreign, even to myself. Waiting for them at home were gardens
to weed, lawns to mow, and family and friends to attend to. Waiting at home for me was all that, plus a mound of placenta-stained
towels to wash, portable fences to move, sheep to chase, lambs to
worry about, and goats to feed. My writing friends were supportive of me as I'd started farming, but I couldn't help but feel
that the more stories I shared with them, the stranger I became,
both to them and myself.

Despite the chaos on the farm, life outside obviously went on
without cutting us any slack. Our bank seemed to be particularly
ignorant of my chaotic life, for they began sending us thin

envelopes. I thought the first was a notice to renew our safety deposit box, so set it aside. Then I received another and another and another, but I put them all on my desk unopened, too exhausted to deal with anything other than this unrelenting birthing process.

After I'd received nine, I realized I'd better open them. All were notices our checking account was overdrawn, and each letter charged us another $15 for a bounced check; $135 in bounced check fees. Cripes.

Off-the-farm pressures affected us both. Melissa's father was getting worse, and there was nothing Melissa could do. She resolved to bring a lamb up to his latest—and hopefully more secure—nursing home as soon as lambing was over. On top of everything else, a tree branch scratched her eye, resulting in a nice corneal abrasion. The eye patch she had to wear for a few days might have been attractive in a pirate sort of way, except that it affected her equilibrium, which meant I'd have to lead her to and from the pasture.

By the time Memorial Day weekend began, I began to see the light at the end of the tunnel. There were only ten pregnant ewes remaining, so hopefully we only had one week left to go. But that Saturday, blustery wind whipped the treetops and the gray sky was heavy with mist. Dread filled me as the rain began. Puddles formed in the shallows of the pasture. It rained and rained. Both of us shrugged on our rain gear and headed for the sheep.

I knew this wasn't going to be a good day, my finely honed sense of dread working beautifully. The one positive, however, was that I noted, through my rain-streaked glasses, how wonderful our new mothers were. They stood in the rain with their lambs huddled next to them, sheltered by Mama's body from the rain as it fell at an angle.

Two new lambs had already been born, but unable to dry off, they stood shivering, hunched over. We took the frail, trembling lambs back up the hill to the house because once they were dried off and warmed up, they'd be better able to withstand the weather. Melissa slid the narrow tube down each throat and I poured in the warm colostrum. We left the lambs in the box in the basement and went back outside into the light but steady rain. A frigid breeze blew from the east, straight across the lambing pasture. Another lamb came, and I took her back up the hill to the house. When I returned, Melissa waved me over.

"Look." She pointed to ewe number 9, with only a lamb's nose and mouth out her vagina. The lamb's tongue was swelling alarmingly, a sign the lamb was probably stuck in the birth canal.

"Great. Now what?" We walked toward number 9. She ran away. We ran after her. My one-eyed pirate fell down and I helped her up. The ewe ran farther away. Water squirted out from under my boots as I ran. This clearly wasn't working.

"Let's net her," Melissa said. We had developed our own technique of catching a ewe by surrounding her with the temporary Electronet fencing. When this ewe tried to run through it, she got hung up in the plastic strands and we wrestled her onto the ground. Melissa put on her plastic glove, and I assumed my position—on my knees, by the ewe's head, holding her down. Then as Melissa slipped her hand inside the grunting ewe, I buried my face against the ewe's neck. The ewe huffed and gave short, confused moans, while I cleverly sobbed into the ewe's wool, my valuable contribution to the miracle of birth. Lordy, but I was a fish out of water. Damn. Why hadn't my parents tried to stop me when Melissa and I had started the farm?

Melissa delivered a huge lamb, the size of some of our week-old babies. Despite her swollen tongue, the little female was strong so we put her in front of number 9. The ewe licked the lamb once or twice, then strained. "Here comes another one," Melissa said. What the ewe ejected into Melissa's hands, however, was not a lamb but a dark purplish-red mass with odd bumps.

"Shit," Melissa said. "I think this is her uterus." A prolapse. Melissa struggled to keep the huge mass off the ground. Rain ran down my back, my knees were soaked as I knelt on the ground. Hands shaking, I helped her raise the ewe's back end, hoping gravity would work with us as we tried to push the uterus back inside. But number 9 pushed against us; her vaginal muscles were too strong. We stared at the swollen organ flowing from the ewe.

"I think we need help," I said.

Melissa nodded. "Do you want to hold the uterus or call the vet?"

"Yeah, right." My feet heavy as bricks, I slogged back up the hill and called the vet. The clinic said all the vets were out, but they'd get to us as soon as possible. I dragged myself back down to the far corner of the pasture. Melissa was leaning over the uterus to protect it from the rain. The lamb, wet and yellow with amniotic fluid, still struggled to stand. I helped her nurse so she got colostrum. While holding the uterus, Melissa pulled off her long glove, turning it inside out so it became a plastic bag filled with the huge dark red organ. She shook out her arm, numb from the strain and I fed her the last Hershey's bar from my stash. Still no vet. The lamb was wet and cold, so I walked back up that blasted hill again to put her under the heat lamp and check for the vet.

The prolapse was an hour old, and still no vet. I could either wring my hands, come unglued, or actually do something useful. That's when I saw the calf hutch. Past exhaustion, I dragged myself up to the fence and shut off the electricity so I could wrestle the hutch over the fences without fear of shock. Made of heavy plastic, measuring six feet across, five feet high, the hutch was awkward and heavy, and moving it was like rolling a massive bowl with square corners, but I somehow got it through the gate and began pushing, shoving, and rolling it downhill.

"Thanks," Melissa said as I dropped the hutch over her and the ewe.

"How are you doing?" I asked as I crouched down by the hutch door.

"Better now." She smiled bravely and even though her lips were blue, her one visible green eye still shone.

"You're enjoying this, aren't you?"

"Well, I'm cold and worried about this ewe, but Cath, look at all the babies we have."

By this time the ewe's eyes were glazed and shocky. Tremors rippled down her side, so I retrieved a blanket and threw it over her. Where the hell was the vet? At least the rain slowed to a drizzle.

Two and a half hours after I called, the vet showed up. The delay wasn't anyone's fault—the office had been swamped with calls—but I was sure the ewe would die. Mark slowly eased the uterus back in, working from the sides rather than the middle, as we had tried. He stitched her up, then trussed her with twine so she couldn't push. Sheep were hardy creatures. When he was done, number 9 stood up, grazed a bit, and bawled for her baby. Bloody and muddy, number 9 made a complete recovery. That afternoon we returned all the bleating lambs from the house to their moms, even number 9. All four took their babies back immediately. Another lamb came later in the day, but that ewe needed no help.

We were both so exhausted we could barely talk. But we had five new lambs, all alive, and five new moms, all alive. To celebrate, we drove into town and ordered a sixteen-inch pepperoni and green olive pizza. The two teenaged boys at the next table ordered at the same time. When both pizzas came, the boys had barely gotten their first slices to their lips before we were finished, wiping our mouths and thinking of ordering another. When it came to food, an exhausted shepherd could beat a teenager any day.

searching for placenta
by moonlight

a **nother lambing day.** As usual, Melissa leapt from bed when the alarm went off that morning. "Babies! Got to go see if there are any new babies!" She stepped into her overalls and rubber boots, grabbed her pink lambing box filled with ear tags, syringes, knives, and marking crayons, and bounded out the door, despite the headache pounding against the inside of her skull.

I dragged myself into my clothes and staggered to the kitchen to turn on the walkie-talkie, our latest development. If she needed me, Melissa would call. Otherwise I could just pace calmly inside the house.

"Goofus One to Base."

"Go ahead."

"We've got a new baby girl. Come see."

I walked down to the edge of the pasture and watched the wobbly lamb nursing, its long tail swishing back and forth.

"Man, that ewe's bag is big for only having one lamb," Melissa said. We searched the ground, and found two placentas, long strings of blood and membrane. "There's got to be another lamb around here." Melissa found her about twenty feet away, in among the trees, weak but alive. While learning to walk, the lamb must have staggered under the fence and into the trees, out of its mother's reach. Unfortunately, by this time the ewe had decided she had only one baby; she wouldn't accept the lamb who had roamed.

All day we watched her butt the hungry, bleating lamb away as if to say, "Go find your real mother." It nearly broke my heart. That afternoon I caught the little one, which Melissa had ear-tagged number 16, and brought her back to the house. She frantically drained the bottle I fed her.

Ewe number 66 gave birth to a sick lamb, which we put under the heat lamp in the basement. Melissa thought 66 had another lamb in her, but when she probed up inside with her gloved hand, she discovered number 66's uterus about to turn itself inside out and pop out the vagina. "It felt like a wet sock," she said later. Melissa instinctively pushed, and the uterus slid back into place.

When I went downstairs that night to feed 66's lamb, I found her dead. I had fed her bottles all day. I had rubbed her head and neck, trying to stimulate her to stand up. I couldn't touch the body, but asked Melissa to take the lamb outside.

Just before dusk, Melissa noticed another ewe in labor, this one with the lamb's head out, but nothing more. The lamb was obviously stuck. I did chores while my mom and Aunt Gladys, visiting to lend a welcome hand, followed Melissa outside to catch the ewe.

The ewe would not be caught, not even with the netting procedure. Soon dusk fell, but Melissa still flung herself across the rough pasture, running in the dark. My mom and aunt finally stopped chasing the ewe, then convinced Melissa to stop as well before she broke a leg. "If you can't catch her, you can't help her," my mom said. By now the lamb's head was swollen with fluid. Sick with worry, Melissa agreed to give up.

Of course 66 was still out on the pasture with a full udder. Melissa was worried about mastitis, an inflammation that could develop if the ewe wasn't milked. Could we try to graft little 16 onto 66? Mary suggested a method for tricking the ewe into accepting the lamb: Find 66's placenta, rub it all over lamb number 16, then see what happens. So at 10:30 PM, with the moon less than a week from full, Melissa returned to the pasture. The ewe with the lamb's head sticking out her back end still stood at the far end of the paddock. Melissa just shook her head.

Amazingly, Melissa knew exactly where the placenta was, and returned with a plastic bag filled with a bloody mass, all the description anyone needs of a placenta. She rubbed some of it over the lamb, now housed outside in the calf hutch, then brought the bag inside and deposited it on the kitchen counter.

"I don't think so," I said as I gingerly moved the bag out into the entryway. I drew a line at placentas on my kitchen counter, one of the few places left where I could actually set and defend a boundary. As for keeping the farm at bay while I slept, no such luck. I could barely sleep that night, worried about the stuck lamb, and about little number 16.

The next morning Melissa took the lamb, darkened with dried blood, and the placenta back out to 66 in the pasture. I waited inside. When I saw her walking back with a lamb tucked inside the front of her barn coat, I knew it hadn't worked.

I leaned my head against the window. Now there would be an orphan in the barn; we'd have to figure out how to raise her. I swallowed hard and pawed through the freezer for the frozen goat milk Mary had given us. On the upside, however, the ewe Melissa and my family had chased the night before was just fine, with a healthy lamb at her side. Maybe all that chasing had knocked the lamb loose. The poor lamb's head was twice the size of a normal lamb, but the vet assured us the swelling would soon go down. Oh, but the sight raised such a feeling of powerlessness in me. Nature was going to do her thing with or without my help or interference; I couldn't control any of it.

Let's see. What had my family said about me and farming? No, I wouldn't think about that.

high anxiety

because anxiety gripped me every day, I'd come to believe that my approach to almost everything on the farm was the better approach, more organized, more efficient, and less chaotic. Less chaos became my life's goal. Unfortunately, the other two members of my ménage à trois did not submit willingly to my well-meaning control. I began feeling like an unpleasant, neurotic person. I wondered if my friends noticed, even though I tried to stay positive. I talked with a therapist about anxiety. She encouraged me to read up on it, to write about my anxieties, to find a way to let go of my need to control everything. She also wondered if I'd been anxious or controlling as a child.

"No," I snapped, then remembered the electric car windows, a neurosis I'd shared with my sister. When I was barely a teenager, my parents bought an Oldsmobile, a huge olive green boat the length of most living rooms. In those days electric windows were the newest rage, so of course the Olds had them. We could only open the windows if the car engine ran.

My sister and I hated those windows. It didn't take us long to figure out that should we be crossing a bridge, and should Dad lose control of the car, and should we careen over the guard rail into the lake or river below, the car engine would die and the power would go off. We would sink like a rock, and would be unable to open the stupid electric windows. We had all this figured out because our family took endless driving trips and we crossed many bridges. We knew the pressure of the water would be too great for us to open our doors, so the windows would be our only hope. We would die horrible deaths because some stupid electrical engineer thought it would be clever to invent electric windows.

We soon devised the only solution. Just before crossing a bridge, we each opened our windows all the way. We did this regardless of season or weather. Freezing temperatures or stinging rain was a small price to pay for a secure escape route should Dad lose control and drive us off the bridge. Mom and Dad would tell us to close the windows, but we wouldn't. We were skilled enough at debate to keep them engaged at least until we crossed the bridge, when we each pushed our little lever, the windows sliding shut.

While I'd never totally shaken my fear of driving over bridges, now the farm provided me with a whole new wealth of worries. The sheep could get out onto the highway and cause a terrible accident. All our animals could become ill and die. Melissa could roll her tractor and be crushed. Friends helping with farming projects could be seriously injured.

I read books on anxiety, I took herbal calming remedies, but nothing helped. I couldn't stop thinking about all the things that could go wrong every day. Horrible images plagued me, and I assumed these thoughts were normal. Some of my fears faded as I learned more about farming, and gained more confidence, but they were usually replaced by others.

Then I found the perfect book for me: *The Worst-Case Scenario Survival Handbook*. I loved the book immediately when I read on the back cover, just below the UPC scanning barcode: "Caution: Book will explode if scanned." These authors understood anxiety.

The book covered every dangerous situation or emergency you could imagine: "How to Escape from Quicksand." "How to Wrestle Free From an Alligator." "How to Jump from a Moving Car." "How to Take a Punch in the Stomach." "How to Perform a Tracheotomy." "How to Land a Plane." "How to Survive if You Are in the Line of Gunfire." "How to Survive if Your Parachute Fails to Open."

Of course, an anxiety-ridden person isn't likely to jump from an airplane, but at least now I knew what to do. If there wasn't another jumper to buddy up with, I was screwed.

"How to Jump from a Bridge into a River" was revealing. Jump feet first, keep body vertical, squeeze feet together—these were obvious steps. But the next one wasn't: clench your buttocks together so water won't rush in and cause severe internal damage. I would imagine the next step, protect your crotch with your hands, accomplished the same purpose.

Somehow, reading about all these potential disasters put my own imagined farm disasters into perspective. The book didn't totally reduce my anxieties, but it made me laugh at them, as did the cartoon with the psychologist telling the patient stretched out on the couch: "You worry too much. It doesn't do any good." The patient's response was "Sure it does. Ninety-five percent of the things I worry about never happen!" Besides, why did I expect my life to be anxiety-free? What if that was all that held me together? Take out the Tin Man's rivets, and what happens?

My absolutely most favorite part of the book was the chapter on "How to Escape from a Sinking Car," complete with illustrations.

Step One. As soon as you hit the water, open your window. Opening the door will be difficult because of the outside water pressure. Step Two. If your power windows won't work (aha!), attempt to break the glass with your foot or shoulder. Step Three. Get out. Step Four. If you are unable to open or break window, remain calm as the car fills with water. When the water reaches your head, take a deep breath and hold it. The pressure in the car should equalize so you can open the door and swim to the surface.

And the best advice of all? "To be safe, you should drive with the windows slightly open whenever you are near water." Ha! Maybe my sister and I weren't so neurotic after all.

Not only had I been right to worry about driving over bridges, I'd also been right to worry about lambing. In fact, so far, I'd give myself a D- grade as a farmer, perilously close to flunking out for the first time in my life.

And if lambing wasn't causing enough anxiety, writing was doing a fine job as well. I'd begun to wonder if I really was a writer. Maybe I was just a lazy person. I just couldn't seem to focus on anything, and I'd recently found rejection letters so discouraging that I decided the best way to avoid these irritating and ego-destroying letters was to never send out any manuscripts. Ha. I'd show those damned editors. Let them just try and reject me without any of my manuscripts on their desks.

having fun yet?

because lambing meant the three *p*'s (pee, poop, and placenta) and all three worked themselves into jean cuffs, socks, and shirt pockets, I was washing clothes, very scary clothes, constantly.

Finally, after 278 loads of laundry, lambing was over. I'd survived, but just barely. Living for three weeks on adrenaline is an amazing experience. Forty-seven ewes gave birth to sixty lambs. Most nursed and lived with their mothers, but I ended up with two bottle lambs, number 16 and another who'd been rejected by her mother. Three times a day I'd warm up the milk in the double boiler, pour it into two sterilized beer bottles, and screw on the nipple caps. Soon the kitchen began smelling permanently of milk; I couldn't get the smell off my fingers. My grandma had called these sorts of lambs "bum" lambs, for in a large range flock like hers, the only way an orphan or underfed lamb survived was to slyly "bum" milk off other ewes. An unsuccessful lamb starved to death unless Grandma saw it in time and brought it up to the ranch house to feed.

We needed milk, so Mary sold us a female goat, a sweet Alpine with black and white markings named Ambrosia. Our hope was that next year she would actually adopt the bottle lambs.

One June morning after the lambs raced to greet me, bleating and pawing at me for their milk, I sat on the straw bale and lowered the bottles. Their tails flicked back and forth as they nearly sucked the bottles right from my hands. I talked softly to the lambs, and when their bellies were full, I picked up number 16 and held her to my chest. She nuzzled through my hair, nibbling at my ear, and I stroked her tight woolen curls. Damn, but they were adorable. Needy and carefree at the same time.

I hated the lambing process, perhaps because birth seemed so close to death. Yet I clung fiercely to this tender animal in my arms, wanting to protect her from whatever dangers lay ahead. I wanted to run screaming from the farm, tell Melissa we must sell it, that we must move to a cramped townhouse in the city and work nine-to-five jobs and battle traffic and crime and long cappuccino lines and have no intimate knowledge of farming, just like normal people.

As I sat there, overwhelmed, number 16, smelling of milk and grass and lanolin, nuzzled my throat. This lamb existed in the world only because we had introduced her dam and sire, and let them do as they would. In a weird sense, I was as much a parent to this beast as were the ewe and ram, and not just because the ewe had rejected the lamb. I felt the same tug for all the lambs.

However, the thought of going through the lambing process again next year terrified me. Yet how could I say to Melissa, "Um, I've changed my mind," and leave her to care for all those babies on her own? My sense of responsibility ran deeper than that. Clearly, the only rational choice was to secretly vasectomize the rams. They'd be shooting blanks, and no one but the vet and I would know. Next May we'd have fifty unpregnant ewes, and I'd just shrug my shoulders and say, "Sometimes these things happen."

Melissa, as planned, put little lamb number 16 in a box, packed up a supply of bottles, then drove to her father's nursing home. If he couldn't come to the farm, she'd bring the farm to him. When she carried the lamb into the building in her arms, few people even noticed, thinking it was a small dog, until the tiny bleating gave her away, and Melissa became the most popular visitor that day. Melissa's father was happy to see the lamb, even though by this time he wasn't entirely sure who Melissa was, thinking now and then since Melissa wore pants she must be his younger brother. Melissa proudly showed off her lamb, and patiently wiped up the messes as the lamb peed repeatedly on the linoleum floor.

That summer Melissa or I moved the whole flock, babies and all, into fresh pasture every day. When I opened the Electronet, the ewes rushed into the new pasture, confident their lambs would keep up with them, or find them eventually. Then we'd stroll through the old paddock, nudging awake any sleeping lambs and trying to herd them in with their mothers. The babies were horizontal firecrackers shooting off in every direction. Run, run, like the wind, their instinct said. It's not important the direction—just run! If we had to catch a lamb to check out a potential problem, it was nearly impossible, so Melissa bought a long-handled net, and we became fairly proficient at fishing for speedy lambs.

Dusk became my favorite time, my reward for the anxieties of lambing, when the rowdier babies formed a gang, racing back and forth across the pasture. One evening the gang hopped from family group to family group, enticing the more timid lambs to join them. Soon forty lambs had joined the gang, leaving only the very young lambs remaining with their mothers, watching with half-envy, half-alarm, as the older lambs romped.

The gang raced to the end of the paddock, then screeched to a halt, eyes wide, tiny chests heaving. One lamb leapt straight up into the air, then another, then another, as if lifted off their feet by tiny explosions. Then one lamb whirled around and began racing back. The flock of babies flowed over the ground's bumps and dips like heavy cream.

Melissa and I sat back on our heels and watched the magic, wishing everyone could see what we saw. These animals were not crammed into a feedlot or a barn. These were happy, joyful creatures.

Of course these delightful evenings only served to confuse me, for while I loved the lambs, I hated what we had to go through to get them. What about some sort of "stork delivery service" for lambs?

LATER THAT WEEK Melissa ran into the house. "I need your help catching a ewe. Looks like she has an abscess on her jaw."

I looked down at my white shorts and pink polo shirt. "But you said you didn't need any help today. I was going to write."

"I know. I'm sorry. But if that abscess bursts, it could infect the entire flock." She wore her now-familiar Angry Face, the one that told me she'd anticipated my must-control-all response, and had been fighting with me long before she stepped into the house. I countered with my equally effective Pissed-Off Face, then tried to convince her the abscess could wait or a vet should deal with it.

Of course this didn't work, so I dragged myself back to the closet, took off my clothes, folded them, and let my fingers brush lightly against the soft fabric. I pulled on my work jeans and a baggy t-shirt with the ragged hem.

We chased the ewe until all three of us were panting. We finally set up a temporary fence and drove her into it. She went down, tangled in the white and orange plastic threads. We caught her, but then had to drag her up the hill to the barn, for sheep will only be led if they've been trained. I stumbled back into the house while Melissa treated the abscess. I threw my muddy jeans down the laundry chute, and collapsed on the bed. Writing would have to wait until tomorrow, again.

Tomorrow came, and Melissa appeared on the front step with a lamb. "Flystrike!" she called. "I know you're writing, but I need your help. I'm really sorry. Here, you hold him while I work on this."

"What's flystrike?" Had I read about this in the books? Melissa snipped off the wool around the lamb's tail and I nearly gagged. White maggots, embedded in the lamb's skin, squirmed and writhed as they were exposed.

"Holy shit," I muttered, trying not to be sick.

"He must have gotten cut or something, then a fly laid her eggs in that cut. The eggs hatched, and the maggots are feeding on him." Okay, now I was going to be sick. The lamb struggled as Melissa worked, so I squeezed him tighter. She used a tweezers to pick out the maggots one by one, dropping them onto the front step, and suddenly I was very busy not only restraining the lamb, but making sure the maggots didn't crawl up onto my boot.

"Having fun yet?" Melissa asked softly as she worked.

"Absolutely." We both held our breath as she sprayed the affected area with this foul yellow stuff that would keep the flies away.

We had to treat three or four lambs for flystrike over the next few days, and each one recovered nicely. And not only that, but I finally had a story idea inspired by the farm. Although, on second thought, "Larry Lamb and the Maggots" sounded more like a punk band than a children's story.

lying through my teeth

people thought it was great we were farming. It gave them a connection to a lifestyle nearly gone in this century, a way to relive memories or visits to grandparents' farms. So I had the following conversation a few dozen times, with friends and new acquaintances.

"How's it going?" a friend would ask.

"Great," I would say. [Note: This is a bold-faced lie. What I meant was: "Terrible. My joints ache all the time. I'm always exhausted. I'm too tired to write, to cook. My life is a mess. I can't stand the chaos. Something is always going wrong. I don't think I'm cut out for this. But my money's tied up in the farm and I don't know how to get out. Help."]

"It must be amazing to be farming."

"Yes, it's wonderful. We're very happy." [Translation: "Actually, some days it terrifies me. I worry Melissa will roll the tractor and be crushed. I worry the sheep will get sick. I worry we'll run out of grass for them to graze. I worry about the new grooves outlining my mouth and forehead. Help."]

"You two are incredible. You knew what you wanted and you made it happen."

"We're good at setting goals, I guess." ["Melissa is the incredible one. I'm the pathetic one. I'm a frickin' bookworm. I never should have agreed to do this. I didn't know what I was doing. Help."]

Then, of course, there were the tedious conversations I held with myself.

"Get out, dummy."

"I can't. She needs me."

"Oh, Queen of Codependency, she had headaches before you appeared on the scene, she'll have them after you leave. You can't change that."

"But she can't do everything alone. We're still getting the farm going, and it's too much for one person. It'll get better. I just need more time."

"Liar. You don't belong out here. Leave, then she'll be free to find someone who *does* belong on a farm, who can help instead of making things harder."

"I can't. Then everyone will know I've failed. I'll have to admit my family was right."

"Big deal. So they find out you're human and screw up now and then."

"But—"

"Does a claustrophobe belong in a cave? No. Should an arachnophobe raise spiders? No. Should an acrophobic live in a high-rise? No."

"Shut up."

"You hate that phrase."

"Shut up."

This was exhausting. Now I was even fighting with myself. Add that to my fights with Melissa, and my life had lots going for it.

We fought about who forgot to close the Electronet tight enough so the sheep broke through (Me). We fought about who forgot to refill the water trough so the sheep were waterless for hours (Me). We fought about trimming sheep hooves so close they bled (Melissa, finally).

Melissa could recover quicker, for two hours after a fight, she could come inside, and drop down into her chair. "Hey, how's it going?"

How's it going? For two hours I'd been languishing on the bed, reliving every angry exchange we'd ever had, dabbing my eyes with a soggy tissue.

The ultimate sign of fury was to sleep apart. On the rare, pre-farm occasions when this drastic measure became necessary, it was understood that the one still in the bed would wait twenty minutes, then shuffle out to the living room sofa and ask the offended one to come back to bed. If there was any unspoken rule in our relationship, it was this. Yet that first summer as fulltime shepherds, the only effective way I could express my outrage and frustration was to sleep on the sofa. Once, twice, three times. Melissa followed the rules each time.

But then one night, after a particularly antagonistic exchange, twenty minutes passed. Then forty. I watched the moonlight cast moving shadows on the far wall. The next thing I knew, I woke up, face chilled from the puddle of drool I'd left on the sofa cushion. I squinted at my watch—3 AM. Boy, she must be really mad. My back ached and my feet were cold. Well, hell, it was my bed too, and a lot more comfortable than this sofa. I threw off the blanket, padded back to bed, lay down carefully, then pulled up the covers, still so blustery with pride I was determined not to touch her. In the dark, Melissa slid a warm arm around me and pulled me into the sleepy curve of her body.

I had fallen in love with Melissa at the beginning of our relationship, and I accepted that as right and normal. But then I *kept* falling in love with her. Talk about unoriginal—other men and women fell in love with different people, but I kept falling in love with the same one.

It was entirely her fault. She'd surprise me with just the right word, or the right smile, and make me laugh when I needed it most, and all the breath would whoosh from my lungs, the ground would open up and I'd fall in, head over heels once again. It was damned irritating.

serge and sonny

While we had concentrated on lambing, the rest of the farm continued to develop. The grapevines took hold, sending up slender shoots that wrapped around the first trellis wire and began reaching up for the second.

The weeds did just as well. Our plan to mow between the rows worked great, so at least once a week I bounced along the uneven ground on the old Ariens mower, my headphones plugged into my Walkman.

The plan for mowing between the vines did not prove to be as successful. I fired up the non-riding mower and began mowing under the trellis wire. Four short passes, then back up and move to the other side of the vine, make four short passes, then move to the other side of the next vine, etc. Because the vineyard sloped, however, I had to pull the mower back up each time, and soon my arms were trembling. After nearly an hour of working on row one, I stopped and looked ahead. One can never appreciate how long four hundred feet is until your sweaty hands clutch the handle of a mower and your shoulders throb and your feet hurt and you realize you will still be mowing when the moon comes up. Then I glanced over my shoulder at the other ten rows behind me, the weeds having shot up ten inches since I'd last looked over my shoulder.

No, the whole mowing-between-the-vines thing just wasn't going to work. The winemaker at the winery we'd contracted with had said, "Weed control will be your biggest problem. You'll have to use Roundup to keep them under control." No, not us. Besides, Roundup was made by Monsanto, which was scaring us with all their genetic crop manipulation. They had come up with a Roundup Ready corn, which meant the farmer could spray his corn with Roundup, killing the weeds, but the corn would survive. I'm sure from a large farmer's perspective, this made weed control much easier, but we were small farmers, sustainable farmers, and we just didn't like the whole idea. Melissa had, however, done some research, and as herbicides went, Roundup was the lesser of all the evils. Once it hit the ground, it bonded to the soil and became inactive, so probably wouldn't harm the environment.

Still, no Roundup for us. We would figure something else out. But until then, our poor little vines would have to make do as the weeds grew and grew, sucking up water and nutrients and sunlight.

We also continued raising meat chickens, and took another batch to the butcher's. The only thing that kept us going through the daily hard work of raising those birds was the response from friends and family—they loved the chicken and wanted more. We would give them more.

Life in the chicken house was never boring, and in the middle of everything else, just after lambing we had to act as mediators when the "rooster situation" occurred. Serge, the polite rooster, developed a foot problem. Sonny, our other rooster (and Serge's son) sensed weakness in Serge and began beating him up because of it, bloodying his comb and pulling out feathers. Serge soon started sleeping in the shed instead of the chicken house, and he'd often hide in there during the day as well.

As the two roosters and the hens roamed around the barnyard, the problem grew worse. Serge limped, and Sonny ran screaming toward his dad. We soon learned to pay attention to the constant crowing contest. If their crows were physically close together, Serge was in danger and we'd rush to intervene. Serge soon learned we were his champions, and the barnyard developed an invisible dotted line, one of the few times a boundary developed instead of disappeared. From the shed to the house's front door, everything west was Serge's territory, east was Sonny's. One day Sonny crossed the line, and flew toward Serge, who raced screaming for the house. Melissa opened the front door and a grateful Serge fell into her arms. It was a little frightening to see such human behavior in animals, until I remember that humans are part of the animal kingdom too, and share many behaviors in common with beasts we consider beneath us.

One day we were too far away to separate the roosters in time; Sonny was on him, literally, while I ran the hundred yards uphill, yelling. When I reached Serge, he was alive but shaken, lying on his side, wings and legs all askew, beak wide open in a dazed pant. I gathered him up, tucked him under my arm, and returned him to the shed. In a few hours he was out again, patrolling his territory.

Melissa was proud of Serge's spunk, and slipped him treats whenever she passed him. Most of the time, however, he turned around and gave those treats away. When roosters find food, they start chortling happily, chicken-talk for "Ladies, come. I have food to share." I once threw old french fries toward a group of hens and teenaged chicks. Serge got there first and snatched up a fry. He chortled to get a chick's attention, then dropped the fry in front of the chick. He did this over and over again, finding the fries hidden in the longer grass, chortling, then dropping them in front of the nearest hen or chick. We'd seen Sonny do the same.

We enjoyed the look on Sonny's face the day we cut up an overripe cucumber for Serge, who chortled loudly enough that all the hens near Sonny dashed over to Serge, the Man of the Hour. Sonny had no choice but to stay in his territory. After finishing the delectable meal, Serge managed to mount two or three of the hens while Sonny crowed in frustration. The old guy still had it in him.

But how long would that last? Some days I felt like Serge, not necessarily weak, but certainly in a war zone. Melissa had always possessed a quick temper, and I had learned to deal with it by walking away, talking calmly, or yelling back. But more and more we seemed to be raising our voices out in the pasture. I couldn't put my finger on any specific reason, but decided it must be the stress from all the changes. Like every other couple, we'd dealt with much over the years—my parents' divorce, job changes, school, moving, new careers—but those conflicts came from outside sources. Now the conflict came from within the relationship. Perhaps Melissa wasn't responding well to my Anti-Chaos Campaign.

Melissa and I talked, and she agreed we'd been fighting more. She took my hand, as she'd done many times before when we'd faced difficulties. "Let's just agree to get through this, okay?"

Okay, I agreed. We were like small matches that flared up but burned out quickly before our anger could do much damage. Besides, life was bound to stretch us uncomfortably while we were still in the middle of such a major enterprise. Starting a farm was just a little bump on the rocky road of life.

A very large bump came later that fall as Melissa's father further deteriorated. We visited him at the nursing home often, even though he was increasingly unresponsive, and we both knew it wouldn't be long.

It wasn't. And even though we'd expected his death, it still rattled Melissa's world, and my own. A neighbor kindly took care of chores so we could spend time with Melissa's family, and at least begin to mourn. The moving funeral ended with a bagpiper playing "Amazing Grace."

let's just forget this
ever happened

the farming cycle continued relentlessly, and we had no
choice but to run to keep up with it. It was time to breed our
female goat Ambrosia, a job Lance and Merlin were unable to perform. Much as I loved them, I began to wonder why we had
Lance and Merlin. If Ambrosia was to give birth to kids next
spring, she needed an intact male . . . now.

For twenty-five dollars, Mary offered her bucks as stud. All we
had to do was figure out when Ambrosia went into heat, then take
her over to Mary's. Female goats cycle every seventeen days or so;
when they go into heat, they are very friendly, rubbing up against
anything, calling loudly in search of a mate. But Ambrosia proved
to be much more coy about these things, hardly saying a word.
We had watched her carefully between visits to the nursing home
and then the funeral.

"Did she seem friendlier today?" Melissa asked, and I marked
it on the calendar. Finally we thought we saw a pattern of seventeen to twenty days between her subtle signals. The next time she
cycled, we'd take her to Mary's.

On schedule, she bleated once during the day. This was it. We
didn't have a trailer, so had to transport her in the pickup. We didn't

have a pickup topper, so couldn't just put her in the back—too dangerous. So two women and a 170-pound goat squeezed into the pickup cab.

At Mary's, we led Ambrosia to the converted chicken house, into a building about twenty feet by ten feet, with bare board walls, its concrete floor dusty with old straw. Mary opened the door and Bozeman came flying in, eyes wild, lip curled at the scent of Ambrosia. Our goat took one look at this creature and began running.

I couldn't blame her. Not only do intact bucks reek with an indescribable scent, but this guy's head and neck were oily, greasy, and matted with something foul. Mary explained that male goats urinate on the insides of their front legs, then wipe their legs over their faces and necks to increase their attractiveness to the opposite sex.

Ambrosia wasn't buying it. Who could blame her? We watched Bozeman chase her in a circle for five minutes.

"Is this how goat sex usually goes?" I finally asked.

"No," Mary said. "Usually the doe stands still. Ambrosia must be near the end of her cycle. She can still get pregnant, but isn't willing to stand still." She sighed. "I'm afraid we have to hold her."

Groaning, we stepped forward. Melissa grabbed Ambrosia's collar but she twisted away. Mary and I cornered her but she slipped past us. Finally it took all three of us to catch Ambrosia. Then, unbelievably, we restrained her head and torso while Bozeman, loopy with lust, flung himself on her and began thrusting his hips.

No one said a word as Bozeman concentrated on the task at hand, and Ambrosia grunted indignantly. I held my breath to avoid Bozeman's aroma. Finally I muttered, "Can I still call myself a feminist after this?"

Mary explained what to watch for next, something about a final thrust, grunt, and a rolling back of the eyes. Bozeman sort of did these things, then dropped back on all fours and walked away. "I don't know if that was a good breeding," Mary said. "Maybe we should try again."

Bozeman was over in the corner lighting up a cigarette, clearly done for the day. "Let's try Palincar." Mary escorted out the smelly Bozeman and brought in a young goat, born earlier in the year. Little white Palincar, hair yellow with urine, trembled with excitement at Ambrosia's scent and flung himself at her.

Mary held Ambrosia's head while Palincar humped wildly. Melissa stood behind Palincar and shifted his narrow hips so he'd at least be in the neighborhood. When it came to mating dairy goats, however, size did matter. Soon we all dissolved into laughter as enthusiastic Palincar thrust his hips repeatedly, his pencil-thin penis trying to impregnate Ambrosia's midthigh. Poor little guy just couldn't reach his target.

So we had no choice but to hope Bozeman did his job. We loaded Ambrosia back into the pickup cab, but unfortunately, she now smelled like Bozeman and Palincar. By the end of the fifteen-minute drive home, so did we.

meeting my meat

fast forward to the early winter. I never got around to having the rams vasectomized, so of course the rams would impregnate the ewes again, those *animals.*

This time Rudy and Otis were really frantic, because they knew what was ahead. We had a new tall, black-faced ram, Andy, a purebred Shropshire; we hoped he'd give us larger lambs. We divided the ewes into three groups, putting the largest ewes with Andy. We let the rams into their respective pens, and whoa boy, what a difference a little carnal knowledge made. All three rams immediately set about romancing the nearest ewe in heat. The chalk markers worked great, and within a few weeks most of the ewes sported blue, green, or red chalk smears on their backsides.

Winter hit hard—howling winds, gray skies, and snow. I spent time in my office pretending to be a writer. We'd moved my office into the loft because in the basement we were framing walls and hanging drywall, learning as we went along.

When she wasn't working in the basement, Melissa spent a great deal of time staring out the window. She'd climb the loft stairs, where I had no door to shut. "We got some snow last night."

"Umhum," I'd reply, knowing it was barely a dusting.

"Maybe I'd better clean off the driveway."

"Melissa, we got less than an inch."

"I'm thinking I should really clear it off. UPS driver might have trouble." She'd plug in the block heater, wait thirty minutes, then fire up her diesel tractor. She'd plow until she couldn't feel her face anymore. Once or twice, after a large storm, she and the tractor would disappear altogether. Just as I'd start to really worry, her headlights would appear at the end of the road. She'd plowed a path for the neighbors to use until the snowplow reached our road.

Action was the only way Melissa knew to deal with everything churning through her, since grief reached out and slapped her in the face nearly every day. I, too, missed her father, his dry wit, that surprising twinkle he'd get in his eye when he was teasing one of us.

But grief or no grief, the sheep needed to be fed every day. One wintery morning, just when I'd decided that of all the seasons on this farm, winter was the easiest because no lambs were born, I came face to face with my meat. It happened the morning I was filling the lambs' water trough, my back hunched against the frigid January wind. While we had sold most of the lambs that had been born in the spring to other farmers to raise, enough family and friends had asked to buy lamb to eat that we decided to finish, or raise to full size, a few lambs. It was one of those lambs, now seven months old, that approached me. I waited, incredulous. Unless they'd been raised on a bottle, lambs wanted little to do with humans. But this one, his black pupils wide, his ears perked forward, touched my extended mitten.

"Hi, cutie," I said and I lightly tapped his wooly head. But instead of running away, he ducked his head shyly, then looked me in the eye. I tapped him again and he ducked again, moving closer. We played our game for a few minutes while the four other lambs in the pen hung back, nervous. But then my hands froze in midair. What was I doing? This lamb was almost ready for market. In one week, this living, breathing, playful lamb before me would be dead—on purpose. I turned away to shut off the water hydrant. "No, no, no," I muttered. "Leave me alone."

But the lamb, now bold, tugged on my barn coat, tentatively tasting the brown cotton. I watched, horrified, as he presented his head for another tap. He couldn't be a pet. He was already slated to be meat. I suddenly noticed his heart-shaped face, the black spots gently splashed across one ear, his perky tail. How could I pay someone to kill him? I tapped the lamb's head one more time, then fled.

Here I was again, meeting my own meat. Of course I knew on an intellectual level I'd be doing this, but when you nuzzle baby lamb noses, when you give them shots, when you bury your fingers into wool slick with lanolin, when you *know* the animals, meat takes on a whole new meaning.

Most lamb we eat comes from animals weighing from 120–150 pounds, nearly the weight of a full-grown sheep. But thanks to Easter and springtime, the lamb is an icon of innocence and youth. Only with lamb does the name of the *meat* match the name of the *mammal*. We eat beef, not cow. We eat veal, not baby calves. We eat pork, not pigs. We eat mutton, not sheep. But when we eat lamb, all that comes to mind is that cute Easter lamb.

During that whole week I tried to avoid the playful lamb, but I couldn't. During my chores he followed me like a puppy, picking up things I put down, tugging on my scarf.

"That's amazing," Melissa said as I showed her our tapping game. She tried it herself. "We shouldn't be doing this," she said.

"I know," I replied, "but I feel like kissing him right on his nose."

"Bad idea," said the woman who repeatedly kissed our ewes, even the ugly ones, as she checked their eyes for inflammations and trimmed their hooves.

Meat comes from animals that have died, plain and simple. How could I reconcile my love of animals with my desire to eat meat?

Some animal rights activists polarize the issue by claiming that all farming is cruel. One group went so far as to release thousands of domestic mink from a local mink farm, thinking they were giving the animals their "freedom." Terrified in unfamiliar territory, the mink were hit by cars, eaten by predators, or starved to death. The lucky ones stayed near the fence until the owners discovered them and herded them back home.

It's tempting to anthropomorphize animals, especially with cute hit movies like *Babe*. But that's a fantasy. Animals aren't human. Temple Grandin, a woman who designs chute systems for handling cattle in slaughter plants, uses her experience as a person with autism to understand the differences between animals and humans. For example, blood horrifies people, but apparently doesn't bother cattle. What makes them nervous are sudden movements, so Grandin designed chutes that cut down on distractions to calm the cattle. When asked how she could care about animals, yet be so involved in their slaughter, Grandin pointed out that domestic farm animals wouldn't be here unless we raised them. She said we owe them a "decent life and a painless death."

The extreme position of some animal rights groups inspires an equally unfortunate backlash that has led to widespread factory farming—the idea that animals don't have feelings, and since they are to be eaten, what does it matter how they are raised? First, animals have emotions. When we have long stretches of gray days, the ewes move slower. When they hear corn being scooped, they race for the barn, and after they're sheared they kick up their heels, energized by an exciting new haircut. Second, *because* we eat animals is precisely the reason why we *should* care how they are raised. After all, you are what you eat.

The playful lamb's "processing" date neared. Only two days left. I searched frantically for alternatives. Could he be a stud ram for us or someone else? I checked the records and discovered the poor guy had only one testicle.

This, actually, was one more than he should have had. Because Melissa was new at castrating those first lambs with the burdizo, her success rate wasn't 100 percent, so we ended up with some males half-intact. A ram needed both testicles to be used for breeding. I was running out of options. Could we keep him for a pet?

I turned to *Playing Ball on Running Water* by David Reynolds for guidance. Some days I could incorporate this book's Japanese philosophy into my life; other days it would have been easier to grab a fistful of water. Deceptively simple, the philosophy could be boiled down to three short sentences: The first sentence was *Accept your feelings.* I thought about the playful ram lamb and knew I would feel great sadness if he was killed. I wanted him to live.

The second sentence was *Know your purpose.* I struggled to put my pain aside so I could think clearly. We raised safe, healthy meat for people to eat. We raised our livestock humanely—the lambs had short but high-quality lives. We were *not* running a dude ranch for sheep, keeping unproductive livestock as pets would soon consume our meager earnings and we'd lose the farm.

The third, and hardest, sentence of this philosophy was *Do what needs to be done.* I accepted my feelings, I knew our purpose, so the next day . . . we did what needed to be done.

We loaded the five sheep into the pickup, a fairly easy task because Mr. Playful followed me up the ramp and the others followed him. We drove the fifteen miles to Cannon Falls in silence. Melissa backed up to the loading dock and we shooed the sheep into the building's nearest open pen. The holding pens seemed calm enough, but my heart raced nonetheless. A huge cow in the next stall sniffed through the rails. Another sheep, freshly shorn, waited in the pen ahead. I wanted to tap the lamb's head one more time, but was too embarrassed to show such affection in front of the man who would kill the lamb. I imagined it would make his job even harder. We closed the heavy wooden door behind us and climbed back into the pickup. Melissa drove around front and went inside to handle the paperwork.

I sat in the pickup and cried. My contacts blurred, my nose filled. Why did I have to face death so directly? Why did everyone else get off free, blissfully ignorant of the death that preceded their meat? I couldn't stop crying. Huge, shuddering sobs. I was still crying when Melissa came out. She held my hand while she drove, and I cried all the way home.

When we brought our meat home from the butcher, there was no way of knowing if it was the playful one, or another of the lambs. The meat stayed in the freezer for a few months until I was ready, then I thawed out some lamb chops.

As we sat down to eat, I discovered an unexpected benefit from meeting my meat, a benefit that reshaped my pain into something worthwhile. On my plate was part of a sheep I'd watched play in the pasture. I took one small bite, then another. The meat was savory and incredibly tender. To honor the lamb that died, I chewed slowly, in no hurry to wolf down the meal. Raising livestock pulled me into a symbiotic, intense relationship with animals: I feed you, then you feed me, my family, my friends. As I ate, a surprising emotion swept through me—deep, deep gratitude.

sexing brenda

melissa bought a white, leggy Brahma hen with black spots, big chest, and absolutely no tail feathers. At her previous home, the poor hen had been pecked naked by the other hens. Unfortunately, our hens began giving her the same treatment, as if they sensed she was already depressed and would be easy to pick on.

Melissa isolated her in a small pen in one corner of the barn, but the other hens started flying over the pen sides for more butt pecking, and the poor hen would hide her head in the corner, leaving her tender, bleeding rump even more exposed.

Melissa totally enclosed her in a safe pen, and came inside to share the good news. "I've got Brenda isolated now so she'll be safe."

"Brenda?"

Melissa blushed. "She seems like a Brenda. Don't know why."

We never named our hens, but that stupid name stuck so firmly even I began to use it. For weeks we fed her separately, sprinkling cracked corn into her feeder, filling her private water dish. She didn't lay any eggs, but we didn't expect her to, given the trauma she'd suffered. Her rump slowly healed, and three scrawny black tail feathers appeared. We started letting her mingle with the other hens, which went well. Emotionally scarred, Brenda continued to hide, but when the border collie came into the barn, she'd stand tall and look him in the eye; she'd follow me around the barn looking for a handout.

One morning after chores Melissa came back inside with a funny look on her face. "I saw Brenda mount a female."

I winked. On our farm this wasn't all that odd.

"Then she mounted another female."

"Can you blame her?" I said.

"Well, no, but it may be that . . ." Melissa stopped and scratched her head, brows furrowed. "I think Brenda might be a Brendan."

That was all this farm needed—another rooster. Since his or her tail feathers hadn't really grown back, we lacked the most obvious way to visually sex a chicken. Roosters have a full, dramatic plume, hens have a modest but thick fan of feathers.

We chuckled over the confusion, but I wanted to know the truth. That night while Melissa worked on our basement project, I tracked down her book, *Sexing All Fowl, Baby Chicks, Game Birds, and Cage Birds.* Apparently this is quite a science; the book began with a riveting account of the history of chick sexing. The Japanese dominated the field from 1925–1932, after which the Europeans took over. In 1935 the U.S. National Poultry Council's Chick Sexing Board even started a certification program. The applicant had to examine four hundred chicks per hour, and identify the sex with 92 percent accuracy. No one passed the first examination; their speed was fine but they made a poor showing of figuring out which birds would crow and which would lay eggs.

Good heavens. What could be so hard about sexing a chicken? After skimming through the book, however, my mind reeled from photo after photo of chicken vents pulled apart to reveal the tiny clitoris, the tiny penis, both about the same size, and nearly microscopic.

About to abandon the book, I found one page that mentioned a sexing device based on the "witching" for water technique. Suspend a small wooden ball on the end of a string over the chick in question. You were not to hold the string yourself, but instead attach it to something, otherwise you might end up sexing yourself, a waste of time for most people. If the chicken is female, the ball will swing in a circle; if male it will swing back and forth. For those without the skills to construct this complex device, an address for ordering one was provided.

On the last page I actually found something useful. Roosters have pointed hackle feathers, those feathers along their rumps, and pointed saddle feathers, those feathers around their shoulders. Hens have rounded hackle and saddle feathers.

I showed the page to Melissa. Within minutes she yanked on her LaCrosse boots and heavy winter coat, then trudged out to the chicken room. She was gone for ten minutes. When she returned, she said nothing while she unwound her scarf, shrugged off her coat, and took off her boots. "Well?" I asked, leaning against the door jam.

"Brendan says hi."

lambing: the dreaded sequel

despite my fervent prayers that spring never come, it did. Our goat Ambrosia was visibly pregnant, her sides stretched and swollen as if pumped full of air. She grunted as she walked, moved slowly, and wore an oddly pensive look. In April, near Ambrosia's due date, we drove to the Twin Cities to have dinner with friends. When we returned about 10 PM, we peeked into the barn and discovered Ambrosia happily nursing three baby goats. Triplets, and all by herself. If all births could be this easy, I wouldn't need my anxieties.

The kids were heart-breakingly cute. Short and slender, they were all dry and fluffy, softer than a lamb. The three does tottered around the pen on wobbly legs. Lance and Merlin stared from their pen, not sure if they approved of this new turn of events. Whenever I had a free moment for the next few weeks, I slipped into the barn and scooped up one of the kids, holding her close to my chest, letting her tuck her head under my chin. Soft, wide-eyed, and intensely curious, the kids put everything in their mouths, tasting my pant legs, my shirt cuffs, my buttons, my chin, my fingers, my hair.

A friend of Melissa's from the vet clinic wanted goats, so she agreed to buy the three kids when we were ready to sell them.

We needed to keep them for awhile, however, so they'd continue nursing on Ambrosia. If we'd sold them before we needed Ambrosia's milk, we'd have to milk her twice a day.

Incredibly, unbelievably, May arrived again. I knew what to expect, so I was even more tense. But I cooked enough lasagna, beef and noodle casserole, French toast, and lamb roast for three weeks and froze it, so at least we could avoid the fast-food burgers. We made a small enclosure in the corner of the goat barn for any newborn lambs who needed to be warmed. I fluffed up fresh straw, relieved the babies would be out here instead of in my laundry room.

I gave up on the idea of writing anything, and asked for three weeks off from my teaching job, since I knew the student assignments were going to pile up anyway. I did not schedule any school visits, bowed out of all meetings, basically clearing a path in my life for Hurricane Lambing.

This time I begged and pleaded with Melissa not to leave the farm. Her job was dispatching the emergency vet, which she did at home. I learned the job so I could spell her during lambing. I'd much rather deal with another farmer's emergency than our own. I did all the off-farm errands. A friend of ours joked Melissa was under house arrest.

Then the first lamb was born. We stood off to one side, grateful it was a warm day, watching as the ewe strained for awhile, then ejected a wet bundle encased in mucus. She turned around and began licking the lamb, clearing its eyes and nose. The feeble lamb lifted its head and bleated. She struggled for a few minutes, but finally stood on wobbly legs. She staggered toward the ewe, reached for the teat, and the ewe stepped away. The lamb wobbled closer. The ewe stepped away. Damn. I was torn between rushing in to help, and letting Mother Nature work things out. Melissa convinced me to relax and just watch. In a few minutes the ewe figured things out and stood still. The lamb banged her head against the udder to get the milk flowing, then her long, wet tail began flipping back and forth as she nursed. I let myself breathe again.

That afternoon we headed outside to check for more lambs. Melissa went up the hill to check on the west batch, and I headed for the east pasture. A tiny bleating floated up from a line of trees, near where the lamb had been born that morning. The ewe was nowhere to be seen. Cursing, I caught the lonely lamb and started walking toward the south, finally coming across the new mother with another group of ewes. She ran toward me immediately when she heard the baby in my arms, as distressed as any mother who'd lost her infant.

After witnessing the happy family reunion, I headed up the hill toward the west to see what Melissa was doing. At the top of the rounded swell, I found a ewe and her two newborn lambs encircled by a short section of Electronet. Two other ewes bleated frantically outside the netting. And if things weren't chaotic enough, alarming black smoke billowed above the neighbor's farm across the road, near where they stored their large round bales. Before I could head for a phone to call 911, Melissa roared down the driveway in the pickup.

I turned my attention to the sheep mess beside me, and soon figured out that one ewe had had twins, then two other ewes both wanted to granny one of the lambs. Melissa had been trying to sort this out when she'd seen the fire. The Electronet physically separated the grannies from their prey, but they were doing plenty of harm with their voices. One would bleat, and the confused lamb would stumble in that direction, bleating. The real mother said nothing. Then the other granny would rush the fence, bleating furiously, and the lamb would stumble in her direction. If I didn't get these grannies out of there, the lamb wouldn't learn to identify its own mother. I ran both grannies off, but they kept coming back, frantic that they couldn't reach what they thought was their baby. The lamb got caught in the netting, which wasn't electrified, as it tried to reach the crying ewes.

So while cars began parking along the road near our pasture to watch the burning hay bales, I ran around the pasture waving my arms like a long-legged windmill, herding the sheep together. The two grannies were swept up in the racing flock, and I chased all the sheep past the new mother, down the hill, and into the holding pen surrounded by an eight-wire fence. The two grannies came racing back but I locked the gate in time, glaring at them and memorizing their ear tag numbers. Those babes were definitely in the doghouse.

Back up the hill, the new mother finally bonded with both lambs. The fire department came to put out the fire, which luckily hadn't spread to the barn or house. I let the rest of the flock out of the holding pen, but kept back the two grannies, who had finally given up their frantic protests. In a few days they'd have babies of their own.

Melissa finally returned, smelling of smoke. We collapsed on the grass, discussing the day. Chaos as usual.

The lambs continued to come. Other than one ewe that needed help, things were progressing much easier than the first year. We were learning to be hands-off shepherds. Not all danger passed once the lamb was born, however. Twice we found week-old lambs dead in the pasture, perfectly fine on the outside. Pneumonia or some other internal disease had proven too much for them. This year most of the ewes had twins; out of the 104 that finally came, we lost 6, not a bad ratio for beginners. Most of these losses, the books told us, were good in the long run, weeding out the weaker genetics. Ahh, genetics. Reminded me of my grandparents' shepherding genes, which *clearly* I did not get.

the goat queen

as lambing progressed, three lambs became orphans all within a day, thanks to mis-mothering, or a ewe unable to feed triplets. I bottle-fed them, then called the woman to come collect the goat triplets. After the kids left, Ambrosia called out plaintively, but luckily replacements waited in the wings.

First, I tied Ambrosia's head and gave her a cup of grain to distract her. Then I knelt, and using my head, pushed the 170-pound goat hard up against the wall. I made sure I was well balanced, for when the grain was gone, Ambrosia would want to be also. Head firm against her flank, I scooped up the nearest two lambs, who were about a day old and a little confused. Sheep udders are high and round, goat udders low and pendulous, so the lambs' instinct to nurse high meant they'd never find the teats without help.

I pushed and pulled the squirming lambs into position, pried open their mouths with a finger, then literally crammed the massive teats into their mouths. Just as I succeeded and both lamb tails were vigorously wagging, Ambrosia got restless so I had to push hard against her with my head. If she shifted, the teats popped right out of those little mouths and I had to start all over again.

The third lamb roamed underneath me, nosing its way up my ribcage, aware the other two were filling their empty stomachs and she wasn't. Even though I wore a sweatshirt, bent over as I was, gravity turns even the most flat-chested of women into a meal source. That third lamb came dangerously close to latching on to exactly what she was looking for, but I pushed her away just in time. As the warning goes: "We're professionals. Don't try this at home."

After the lambs nursed three times a day for three days, Ambrosia's milk passed all the way through their digestive systems, so both ends of each lamb smelled familiar (to her, not to us). The next morning I looked out the window—there she stood, munching her cud, with three little lambs fighting over her udder. They began following her everywhere. She nickered if she couldn't see them. She lay down and let them climb on her . . . a happy blended family.

Two days later we had two more bottle lambs. Ambrosia wouldn't have enough milk for five lambs, so we bought five-year-old Taffy from a woman near Red Wing. Taffy was caramel, with a massive cocoa-brown udder.

I began with Taffy the same procedure I had successfully used with Ambrosia. Three days, four days, five days, Taffy continued to refuse to stand still for the lambs unless I tied her up and forced her up against the wall three times a day.

After seven days, every encounter left me exhausted and frustrated. Goats have a strong sense of hierarchy, so I scolded Taffy, "I'm the boss. Just ask Lance and the others. Now cooperate." No luck. Once again Taffy butted the lambs away as they frantically sought her udder, so once again I had to tie her up and push her massive bulk against the wall.

The thought of doing this for another month until the lambs were old enough to wean horrified me. Over a week and a half had passed, and Taffy was still uncooperative. I tried pleading. I tried the gentle approach, thanking her each time she "donated" milk to the lambs. Other times I cussed impatiently and Taffy would grunt, kick, but not acquiesce.

The two lambs raced for Taffy every time I tied her up. They lost no time in butting the udder, then sucking fast and furious until their little sides bulged out like cantaloupes. She wouldn't let them nurse unless I forced her to. Finally one day I gave up, announcing to Melissa that Taffy was now her problem, then hopped into the car to run some errands. As I drove away, if that goat had had a middle finger to show me, I'm sure she would have.

An hour after I left, Melissa witnessed Taffy standing outside the barn, calm, placid, letting the lambs nurse. No doubt who was boss in *this* herd.

drowning in dreams

We slept like the dead every night, except for an occasional nightmare. Now and then Melissa would wake us both with a sharp cry and a violent jerk that shook the bed. We lay there in the dark, both our hearts pounding until she could find her voice. "Sorry. I touched the electric fence."

Still sad and angry over the loss of her father and worn down by headaches, Melissa struggled every day to prove herself, to make our farm productive and useful to the world. She wanted the farmers she knew to be proud of her, to accept her, to see her as an equal. She was torn daily between working on the farm, and driving up to the Cities to help her mother cope with her new life.

As for me, I was haunted by the recurrence of an old dream I'd had before we moved from the city. I don't usually remember my dreams, basically because they're boring, and truth be told, I'm not all that interested in other people's dreams, either. But this one haunted me. I walk up to the ocean's shore, drop my clothes in a pile, then walk across the packed sand beach into the cold surf. I wade out deeper and deeper until my head disappears under the waves. I never surface. End of dream. Whoa.

MY DOG TORY was both smart and gentle. Her long cocoa-brown hair flowed when she ran, especially her full-plume tail and long ears covered in gentle curls. But at eleven, Tory was wasting away. Her mind, heart, lungs, and kidneys, etc. all worked fine, but her worn-down dysplastic hips ground into her hip sockets with every step she took. She was on horse-strength pain pills. I had one vet implant tiny gold balls around the hip joints, balls that, when stimulated electronically with acupuncture needles, eased the pain. Another vet injected a Novocain-type drug into similar pressure points. But it got harder and harder for her to climb stairs. She walked up the shallow landscaping stairs with me one afternoon and a back leg slipped off the stair. Her whole back end collapsed; she could do nothing but wait as I ran to her and lifted up her back end. Uncomplaining, she limped every night as she walked toward the bedroom.

We joked about making Tory a sling on rollers for her back end, teaching her to scoot about. I was prepared to help her stand whenever necessary, to help her outside and back in, but I wondered how far things would go, and if I'd have the courage to make a decision when that time came. Now and then I would look at her emaciated hips and my heart would jerk, as if hit by the fence in Melissa's nightmare.

BAD DREAMS HAVE a way of leaking into the light, so I soon began each day with vivid images of what might go wrong today. Melissa crushed by the tractor. Melissa cutting off her leg with the chain saw. Me poking my eye out with a tool. Hey, even though my energy to write had dried up, at least I was still using my creativity.

My imagination drove me crazy, so I questioned everything Melissa did. "Do the sheep have enough pasture?"

"Yes."

"The grass looks short. Shouldn't you move them?"

"Okay."

The anxiety wheel would churn harder. "But maybe if you do that, we'll run out of pasture too soon."

She'd throw up her hands, and snap at me.

Other fights came about when Melissa found herself in a situation where I'd nagged her before. I didn't even have to be in the room for her to work up a head of steam, repeating the same argument. Then when I did walk in, she'd blow up and I wouldn't have a clue a fight was already in progress.

Melissa knew I was miserable. I discerned this because many of our fights began with Melissa's anguished growl, "You're miserable!"

"I am!"

"Then we have to sell the farm—the sheep, the goats, the land—everything." Total anguish.

"Don't be so black and white. I just can't seem to write any more. I don't know whose fault that is." Actually, I knew it was mine—I was an average, uninspired writer. I was lazy. Women with families wrote all the time, so what the hell was my excuse?

We both grew weary of the constant shouting. Sometimes I would just walk away, but other times I stood and gave it to her right back. I wondered how much the neighbors could hear. Sound carries.

I still loved this woman. But I didn't understand why we couldn't stop yelling at each other. I tried to be patient as she worked through her grief, but something more was going on. One day we had a huge fight, the same one we'd been having for months about how my way of doing something was a shortcut to be scorned, and her way was the only way. (I've been told this is a common belief of Germans, especially a German born as an Aries—their way is the only way.)

My heart hardened. I was sick of this, so made a list of what I would bring with me in a new life: Tory, my piano, my books, my computer. I bought a Rochester paper and looked in the Apartments for Rent section. None of the apartments allowed pets, but even if I were lucky enough to find one that did, it must be on the first floor because of Tory's hips.

I was through with this sick little ménage à trois. Melissa and the farm would be very happy together without me.

Then the next day we were laughing, teasing and flirting and talking, and I wondered what my problem was. Our days were filled with work and friends and possibilities. Our nights were filled with 8,000-volt electric fences and a drowning woman.

coyotes and paper plates

One late June morning when the lambs were still young, a new mother filled the small valley with thin, confused bleats. When no answering call emerged from the pile of lambs sleeping under the trees, we started searching through the long, dew-heavy grass. The week-old lamb was probably asleep somewhere, curled up and oblivious to her mama's call.

I found her in a small nest of flattened grass. Her head, neck, shoulders, and front legs, were perfect, except for two teeth marks along the throat. I stared at the floppy ears, willing them to twitch in the cool air. But they couldn't, because the back half of the body was gone, severed by canine incisors above the ribcage. My stomach lurched at the violence.

It had to be a coyote. A dog wouldn't have been so neat. Feral and domestic dogs kill for sport, so would have wreaked more havoc among the flock. The coyote slipped under the fence, slunk to the nearest sleeping lamb, killed it with a bite to the throat, took what it wanted, and left. The farm's fence was the only boundary I had left, and now even that had failed me. Coyotes were a menace, but better than wolves because wolves are protected, even if they were destroying a farmer's flock. At least having coyotes meant we didn't have wolves in the area. If wolves ever showed up, the coyotes would take off.

Melissa disposed of the body while I stomped back to the house, my fury overtaking my shock. How dare a coyote sneak in and kill one of our lambs. All my anger and frustration at how the farm had battered away at my writing funneled itself into such a fierce need to protect that I considered camping out in the pasture. Fantasies involving guns and coyotes hounded me all day. In one, it's near midnight as I wait crouched in the pasture, my rifle resting lightly in my hands. The breeze blows the grass into imagined predators, but I am calm. A brief parting of grass near the fence, then a massive coyote, gray in the moonlight, leaps over the fence toward my vulnerable sheep. In one fluid motion, mercury rising, I stand, raise the rifle, capture the coyote's chest in my sights, and pull the trigger.

This was clearly a fantasy, for the chances of this gun-phobe hitting anything weren't good. My only target practice was the spring afternoon Melissa nailed four white paper plates to a large piece of plywood.

"Come on," she said. "You need to learn how to shoot." We stood on the front step with the skinny little .22 Bearcat Melissa had used as a kid. She showed me how to nestle the gun's stock up against the hollow in my shoulder.

I looked down the slender barrel, closed my eyes, braced for the kickback, and squeezed the trigger.

Bamm! Right into one of the paper plates. Not the one I was aiming for, but so what?

"Wow," Melissa breathed. "You hit the plate. Try again."

Bamm. I killed another paper plate, then another, then another.

Then Melissa fired five bullets into the plywood, missing the plates, all four of them, every shot.

"Now my turn," I said. I hit the paper plates over and over again. Then Melissa hit the plywood, over and over again.

"Gosh," I said, "this is fun. Hand me more bullets."

"No, that's enough," she said. "We're wasting ammo."

My sharpshooting skills were ironic, since I didn't like guns. I was a liberal, and I wore Birkenstocks, with socks even. But by the end of the day that I'd found the dead lamb, my need to kill had only grown. I wished we had something more powerful than the Bearcat. The next week when we visited the new outdoor superstore in Owatonna, I was drawn to the racks and racks of guns, their glossy brown stocks and gray barrels glimmering in the fluorescent light. Lined up against the counter drooling over these guns were about twenty men, and me.

My eye was drawn to the Lightning Fire Fluted Rifle with musket cap ignition, guaranteed to be five times hotter than standard number 11 caps, and was tested at over 2100 FPS. Wow. I didn't know what FPS meant, but 2100 seemed high. Or perhaps the steel gray Buckhunter Pro In-Line Rifle, with fully adjustable rear sight, beaded-blade front sight, PVC ramrod, and recoil-absorbing rubber butt pad. That last feature confused me a little, so I gave up trying to visualize it. I liked the look of the nifty little BSA Super Star Mk2, with a patented rotary breech loading system, a manual safety, and coolest of all, an automatic anti-beartrap.

I left without buying a rifle. I had to face facts. Unless a coyote stood stock-still and made like a paper plate, he had nothing to fear from me. Besides, the desire to protect our place with guns could have gotten out of hand. See a coyote? Bam! See a raccoon stealing eggs? Bam! See a skunk stealing eggs? Bam! (On second thought, that wasn't a good idea.) See a stray dog killing chickens? Bam! A robin taking a worm? A hummingbird taking nectar? Bam, Bam!

Obviously I had to temper this urge. Even if I had the equipment and the opportunity, I doubted I would shoot a coyote. Besides, hanging out in the pasture every night with a loaded gun just wasn't an option. There were other ways to discourage predators without bullets, a strong fence being the first. We had a five-wire electric fence made of smooth, high-tensile wire, but the power was being temporarily drained off by weeds, so the fence lost its ability to deter and the coyote didn't hesitate to risk a small jolt for a meal.

Other farmers used woven wire fences, which were strands of wire, not electric, laced with eight-inch square openings. We'd heard too many horror stories about sheep getting their heads stuck in the fence and dying. Of course our sheep never went more than twelve hours without one of us checking on them, but we couldn't stand the idea of finding a dead sheep in our fence. Some farmers still used barbed wire, but only because those fences had been built years ago.

"We could get a guard dog," Melissa said. Some farmers used guard dogs, usually massive white Great Pyrennes or Marcmma, that lived permanently with the flock. The dogs must bond with the sheep as puppies. No one predator control method was foolproof, however. One shepherd we knew had a guard dog, yet still had to walk the perimeter of her pasture every night, moving lambs who'd settled down too close to the fence.

"I think a llama would be fun," I said.

"We could get a donkey," Melissa said. "Paul and Lela might have an extra one." Donkeys were too much like horses, which scared me as much as huge cattle.

"I think a llama would be fun," I repeated.

"Maybe a guard dog and a donkey," Melissa said.

As we talked I thumbed through the latest Cabela's catalog, flipping straight to the gun section. "I've got it. Here's what we do. We buy a Crosman 1008BG." I showed Melissa the photo of the pistol, a stupid choice for hunting coyote, but after reading the description, it seemed the perfect gun for me. With the pistol you got two hundred fifty .177 caliber pellets, four easy-loading eight-shot pellet cylinders, three CO_2 powerlets, and best of all, three paper targets.

"Okay, a llama it is," Melissa said.

Yes. I'd lost so many arguments as we had birthed the farm that I was pleased to have won this one.

the sixteen-inch llama

all the books said the llama's presence alone was supposed to scare off coyotes. Protective and curious, llamas would investigate anything new in a pasture, such as an uninvited coyote, who, once detected, was supposed to slink off into the night. If predators did venture into the pasture, a llama would charge, swinging his powerful long neck like a battering club.

I dug through my files for the llama farm brochures I'd collected at the state fair the year before. A gelded male seemed to be the common recommendation for guarding sheep; intact males had been known to try to mount ewes, which left a pasture full of ewes with broken backs. A llama would eat whatever the flock ate, so feeding him would be easy. A few phone calls found us a gelded llama only fifteen miles away. Fancy stud males could cost ten thousand dollars or more, but gelded, or castrated, males were affordable; this one was four hundred.

The owner of the buff-tan llama held his head so we could approach him. His liquid black eyes, hooded with long, black lashes, blinked occasionally. His upper lip separated in the middle to now and then reveal long, yellowish teeth. I reached for his soft, fluffy coat, but he danced away, surprisingly delicate for a three-hundred-pound animal. You could look, he said, but don't touch.

The owner delivered Moche a few days later. One of the first things Moche did out of the trailer was relieve himself. We stood for nearly five minutes as he emptied his bladder, his relationship to the camel family suddenly clear. While we waited, Melissa had plenty of time to notice that he peed backwards, between his legs, rather than the way most four-legged males pee, shooting forward.

We kept Moche separate at first, hoping he'd bond to us, but he wanted nothing of it. He paced the fenceline of his pen, staring off toward the flock, wearing the grass down to bare earth.

Finally we let him in with a small flock of ten ewes and their lambs. What would this massive animal do around fragile lambs? He surprised us by approaching each lamb slowly, stretching out his neck to smell the baby. The sheep soon accepted his presence so we put him in with the entire flock. Because his coat was light, he blended in well, only his great height and alert, upright ears giving him away.

To find out why our llama peed backwards, Melissa poured over the llama book she borrowed from the vet. After a night of sitting before the computer, not quite writing, I staggered down the loft stairs, heading for bed. Melissa met me at the bottom of the stairs. "Did you know a llama's penis is sixteen inches long?"

I rolled my eyes. "And thank you very much for tonight's nightmare."

"And it swivels."

I sighed. There was no way I was getting to bed without hearing why a llama penis swivels.

"Remember I said he pees backwards?" she said as she searched the book for the correct page. "You want to see a photo?"

I firmly closed the book. "You want to sleep on the sofa?"

"Right. Okay, well, anyway, it points back between his legs when he pees, but when he breeds, it swivels forward so he can mount the female."

"Very cool," I said. "Can I go to bed now?"

Even though I gave Melissa a hard time, it was exotic and exciting to own a llama. Our first clue that Moche, sixteen inches and all, had bonded with the flock came the day Melissa moved the sheep to a new pasture, but Moche stayed behind, laying on top of a small earthen dam. Melissa went back to get him, and discovered twenty delinquent lambs goofing around down behind the dam. Only when she shooed them up over the hill and toward the main flock did Moche stand, survey the area for stragglers, then regally follow.

Our farm was full of places where, if a lamb didn't pay attention and follow the flock, she could end up on the wrong side of the fence, and sheep hate that. All they want is to be with other sheep. Trying to herd young lambs separated from the flock is nearly impossible—they don't respond to any of the usual tricks, but just run willy nilly all over the place. As our friend Joe said once, "You'd almost wish the whole flock would get out rather than just one."

One day Melissa moved the sheep out of a series of pens, but a bunch of lambs got confused and ran back into a pen instead of out into the pasture. Before Melissa could get to them, Moche doubled back, entered the pen himself, and herded the lambs out into the pasture.

Another day when we moved the sheep, one lamb took a wrong turn, finding herself in a dead end, surrounded by electric fence. Moche stayed with the lost lamb until I had time to double back and drive her in the right direction. By that time, the flock was on the other side of the woods, so the lamb couldn't see them. She panicked, took another wrong turn, and blasted through a three-wire fence. Once a sheep's vulnerable, exposed face gets past an electric wire, her wool protects her from further shocks as her body flies through the fence. Moche waited until both Melissa and I were on the job, then he ambled off to join the flock. We succeeded in moving the lamb close enough she and her mother could communicate, but they were still separated by a three-wire fence. Having gone through one, the lamb was clearly reluctant to go through another. We ran back and forth, but the lamb wouldn't move toward the opening that would let her into the paddock with the rest of the flock. It was 7 AM. Sweat ran down my back and neck as we chased the lamb back and forth.

Then Moche reappeared, rolling his massive eyes at us. Really, he seemed to say, can't I trust you women with even the most basic of tasks? He walked along the fence, stopped when he reached the lamb, then led her down through the gate where she gratefully bounded over to Mom and began nursing. Moche wandered off to munch on the box elders. I felt as stupid as the fence post next to me.

Turns out Moche was not only good for predator control, he was also a nanny and a herder, gently watching over his babies. We didn't lose any more lambs that year, either because Moche discouraged predators, or because the fence was stronger, or the predators had left. It didn't matter why, but we slept much easier, confident Moche was on the job. Good thing I wasn't the jealous type, because our llama was a much better shepherd than I was.

the only good goose
is a dead goose

the weeds in the vineyard could now qualify as trees. We *had* to figure out a weed control method we could manage, so I wrote a grant proposal to the Minnesota Department of Agriculture's Sustainable Ag Program. My rusty writing skills did the trick, for we received a small grant to conduct a three-year study to determine the best nonchemical weed control method in a commercial vineyard.

We proposed to split the vineyard into four sections, where we would test four methods. The first was flame weeding. We'd read that strawberry growers were successfully using propane torches to blast the weeds off the face of the earth. Melissa especially liked this idea, and looked forward to a rewarding pyro experience, so we purchase a propane tank, a small two-wheeled cart for pulling it through the vineyard, and a long-wanded torch. We tested our fire extinguisher to make sure it worked, just in case.

The second method was wool mulch. We'd read about this exciting product and thought it made sense for a farm that produced wool. The commercially produced mulch came in rolls three feet wide and about fifty feet long. It was about a quarter-inch thick, and looked like a rough brown wool blanket. We would lay the mulch down, cutting it into sections to fit around the vines, then attach it to the ground with six-inch ground staples.

The third method was similar, but was a black synthetic fabric supposed to be an effective weed barrier.

The fourth method nearly brought tears to the eyes of my beloved poultry addict when I suggested it: geese. The honking beasts had been used by strawberry growers and some vegetable growers to weed their patches. Melissa thought life just could not get any better if we actually could own chickens and geese. She immediately ordered twelve young Toulouse goslings.

As a writer, I did a great job on our proposal. What I sort of forgot, however, was that someone would actually have to provide the labor to lay the two mulches, torch the weeds, and keep the geese under control.

Luckily we were blessed with friends and family who, regardless of what they secretly thought of our farming venture, were willing to help us out. So we had a few mulching parties, where everyone spent the day on their knees, cutting back the existing weeds, measuring and cutting and stapling the mulch. My knees don't mind being used for walking, but they don't appreciate holding all my weight, and quickly let me know this.

With help, we were able to get most of the black mulch section done, and about two-thirds of the wool section. Good enough for now.

Our proposal was to monitor the four methods over three years for the most effective weed control. In three months we had our answer.

Melissa began the flame weeding. The first row was fun, but then the propane tank started to weigh about four hundred pounds as she dragged it along the bumpy ground. The longer the weeds, the longer it took to flame them, until she was using almost an entire tank just to do one row. The time and propane required were just too great. She had too many other things screaming her name, and the torching project fell by the wayside.

The wool mulch was about as effective as a piece of tissue paper. Not only did the weeds come shooting through the mulch, but the thirteen-striped ground squirrels (sort of a little gopher) took up residence under the mulch, digging burrows and swelling the mulch to the point of bursting with their nests and piles of soil. One afternoon I walked down a row with a stick and poked a swollen section of the mulch. Something underneath squeaked back.

We complained to the mulch people, who explained we should have put the mulch down on bare ground, but the only way we could have gotten bare ground was to use Roundup. Not on *this* farm.

The geese did great, for about a month. They ate the weeds, crapped all over everything, and honked whenever we appeared. But after a month in the vineyard, they got bored with the grass and began eating the vines, killing six. That was it. End of the Geese Method of Weed Control.

Expelled from Eden, the geese took up residency in the pasture and immediately identified every gate I used. They then hung around each of these gates, creating two problems. First, they deposited an obscene amount of goose droppings everywhere I needed to step, long, thin white pencils of poop, moist and squishy and smelly. Second, the geese were, to put it mildly, hostile, stretching out their necks to hiss at me and flapping their wings threateningly. Melissa thought it was funny, but it wasn't her they were harassing. We started fighting over the geese. I threatened to wring their necks, use them for target practice, anything to get them off the farm. But Melissa resisted, and the geese stayed.

The fourth method, the black mulch, did amazingly well, especially the parts I did not hit with the riding mower and chew up into tiny black bits that blew through the vineyard. It kept the weeds down. But how on earth could we install the mulch in the rest of the vineyard? Time stalked us. We were still building fences, laying water lines, fixing things, and learning how to keep sheep alive and healthy.

Yet every spare minute not spent with sheep or chickens or goats, that one-acre vineyard was yelling, "Hey! Over here! What about me?" I began hoping I might go insane so I could check into a psychiatric unit down at St. Mary's and be free of all this responsibility.

if it's in a book,
it must be true

i started reading books by other women who'd started farming. In *Sheep in the Corn, Eggs in the Coffee,* a delightfully calm
woman looked back on her seventeen years as a farm wife. She
only lost her temper once. That didn't sound healthy.

In *Shepherdess,* the author shared her mistakes, and they made
me feel better. But she only had five sheep. Because she didn't have
a clue what real trouble was, it felt good to feel superior to her
and sorry for myself.

In *Fifty Acres and a Poodle,* the author described how she and
her fiancé-then-husband bought fifty acres, moved into the country, and called it a farm. I enjoyed the book, but I wasn't sure one
could really call the author's place a farm, for there were no crops
cultivated and the only livestock on the place were their two dogs.
Besides, if you owned a poodle on a farm, should you really be
admitting this to the rest of the world? I think not.

In *Real-Farm,* the author and her husband moved out into the
country, and while they also did not have livestock, they struggled
with an old well, a windmill, and for some unknown reason,
bought geese. Then halfway through the book, the husband just
disappeared. The author discretely referred to her divorce, then

kept on about the farm, and how living in the country had changed her perceptions of everything. I wasn't expecting a Jenny Jones/Jerry Springer sort of confession, but couldn't she have at least given me a few details? Did she and her husband perceive the farm differently? Did the farm cause them to perceive each other differently? What had gone wrong?

I imagined the author and her husband must have fought over their geese. Perhaps he cried, "It's me or the geese," and suddenly found himself renting a one-bedroom apartment in the city. Geese were definitely bad news. I wondered if any relationship could survive geese.

Books by other farmers were of little help. I read books on relationships, but they were no help. Maybe I was in the throes of a midlife crisis, so I read books on turning forty. No help. Yet I continued to comb the self-help aisle of every bookstore I entered. *How to Communicate More Effectively.* No. *Get Out of Your Own Way: Overcoming Self-Defeating Behavior.* A possibility. *Living with Anxiety.* No. I wanted to eliminate anxiety, not invite it into my life and encourage it to get cozy on my couch. *The Meaning of Dreams.* No. *Unleash the Powers of the Unconscious Mind.* Yes, if this meant I could stand in the pasture and use my unconscious mind to send messages to the sheep: "Please don't have sex with the ram this winter—hold out, use some self-control, consider family planning. If you lived in China you'd be done with this whole thing." *Emotional Vampires: Dealing With People Who Drain You Dry.* Now we were getting somewhere. A vampire farm ... no, vampire sheep. Vampire goats. Little yellow ducklings with vampire teeth.

Unbelievably, none of the books explained how a nearly-forty lesbian in a long-term relationship could (1) extricate herself from a farm, (2) find her writing voice, and (3) stay in the relationship, which just showed how out-of-touch publishers are with today's world, that they would leave this vital gap unfilled.

But then one day in a rare day off the farm, browsing through the Walker Art Museum's bookstore, I picked up a book on, of all things, tattoos. Melissa had recently met a fascinating woman coroner who collected photos of tattoos; in her business she saw hundreds. My ranching cousin had acquired tattoos snaking up both arms during his stint on a Navy aircraft carrier in the Far East. Another cousin had his frat house symbol tattooed on his ankle.

The book said most people got tattoos to mark a transformation or transition in their lives, to celebrate some major change or event, to honor making it through something.

That was it! My answer lie not in a book, but in a tattoo. I wanted out of this mess in which I'd ensnared myself, I wanted to be through the uncertainty and fights and over-developed sense of responsibility and unhealthy stubbornness. A tattoo would symbolize this transition, this transformation into a new life.

I closed the book on tattoos and put it back on the shelf. Wishful thinking, and premature. I hadn't gotten through anything. I was still teaching, a job that had become increasingly difficult and one that likely interfered with my own creativity. The course's first assignment was to write a short story based on one of three drawings. The goal wasn't an original story, but just to get people writing. One drawing showed a mother rabbit in the kitchen baking pies, and a young rabbit outside running away with a pie. After reading the 399th story about Floppy the rabbit stealing the carrot pie and learning that stealing was wrong, I began to bang my head against the desk.

Another drawing was of two children running toward a barn, thunderclouds hanging ominously overhead. I read what felt like thousands of stories about two children running to the barn to escape the storm, where a baby cow/horse/sheep was then born, which the children almost always named Stormy. The writers had clearly never actually witnessed an animal birth because the births in the stories were, without exception, blood-free, fluid-free, stress-free. The farmer always delivered the baby as nonchalantly as I'd deliver a pizza.

It was becoming increasingly difficult to find something original, or even kind, to say to my students. And when it came to writing my own stories, my head was so full of carrot pies and baby calves named Stormy that I couldn't hear anything else.

I was still struggling to be a farmer. Melissa and I were still fighting. I was still a lazy, unfocused writer. No, a tattoo wasn't appropriate when my future was as muddy as our barnyard.

mermaid dreams

even though I really no longer wrote, I still spent my annual week on an island on Rainy Lake with my children's writer friends, where I soaked up the sun, ate great food, and pretended to still be a writer. I stunned myself the afternoon I actually wrote something: a scary piece about a woman who walks naked into the ocean, becomes entangled in the seafloor kelp, and drowns. Lovely. That was all I needed—more drowning images. When the woman comes to, she's breathing water through gills and has a tail. Weird. Weird. Weird. A mermaid? What the hell did that mean? Transformation? But half of her stayed the same, so she was half woman, half fish. A mutant. She didn't really belong fully in either world.

In a way, that had always been me. Sometimes I wondered if I'd agreed to farm because I'd always wanted to be a cowgirl, and sheep and my grandma's ranch and cowboys were all mushed together in my head. I have a photo of me at age three wearing jeans, a black belt with Western buckle, and a red cowboy hat. Over the years I collected horse statues, and plastered my walls with horse posters. I read *Black Beauty* and *Misty of Chincoteague* until I knew them by heart. My grandmother's ranch in Montana was exotic to this city girl from Wisconsin. We'd visit her every year, but she didn't have horses, so we'd drive sixty miles to visit cousins Audrey and Byron.

When I was ten, Audrey saddled her horse Blaze, and I boldly mounted for my first riding experience. The horse immediately took off with me, zigging and zagging through a field of sharp, rusty implements. Somehow I stopped the horse, but not before providing a life's worth of entertainment to my cousins.

Years after my memorable ride on Blaze, I asked a friend to teach me to ride. I overcame my fear and learned to control the horse. I liked the experience, but my body didn't. After an hour of riding, when I slid from the huge beast my knees were numb and couldn't hold me up. My hips felt like I had just delivered the horse, not ridden it. No, I wasn't a cowgirl. And I certainly wasn't a farmer.

When I returned home from my writing week I showed the piece about the mermaid to Melissa. "What does it mean?" she asked as we sat on our new porch swing, which was more accurately called a "yard swing" because we didn't have a porch.

"I don't know."

Melissa leaned forward, planting her boots on the ground and her elbows on her knees, bringing a harsh end to the swinging. "You're writing about drowning. I think it's clear. You're miserable. You can't write. This isn't what you want. I hate it that you're unhappy." She pulled off her cap and ran her fingers through her hair, not looking at me. "Maybe we should sell the farm."

I let my breath out like a slow leak. "What would you do if we did?"

She turned, alarmed. Terror didn't just flicker through her eyes, it took up permanent residence. "I don't know," she whispered. "This is the only thing I want to do." I could barely hear her now.

The ocean liner surged ahead, taking up slack so the dinghy could once again feel secure. "We can't sell the farm," I said.

Melissa leaned back and the swing began swaying again, but neither of us was satisfied with our conclusion, or lack of it. It truly haunted Melissa that her dream had totally erased my own. Ironically, our sense of responsibility and stubbornness, our fear and uncertainly, and above all, our exhaustion, blinded us to an obvious solution. We owned a copy of *Wine for Dummies* and *Windows for Dummies*. What we really needed was *Problem Solving for Dummies*.

That summer I had dinner with Marion, my mentor and first writing instructor, during which I shared my insecurities and writing woes. What a whiner I was. Marion was kind but firm, announcing that I did not have her permission to quit. Great words, but too late. I wasn't a writer any more.

So I ignored Marion's advice and drove home, shrugging off my faux-writer's beret and pulling on my farmer's cap. Despite my exhaustion, every time I drove into our driveway I could look around and see we had created something amazing. We had a one-acre vineyard, or rather, a one-acre patch of weeds masquerading as a vineyard. We had lots of healthy sheep and baby lambs. We had chickens who laid delicious eggs.

We had raised, by now, over 450 meat chickens. I wondered how much money we'd made off this venture, so Melissa sat down and added up all the costs of feed, building and maintaining the pens. I added up all the hours we spent moving the pens, a laborious task that had begun to exhaust both of us.

Turns out we were not making a profit on the chickens. We weren't making anything but more work for ourselves. To my surprise, Melissa suggested we give the broiler chicken part of our operation a rest. We quietly dragged the pens behind the shed and left them there. We weren't the only ones—soon farms all over the area were littered with abandoned portable pens.

Our coyote-prevention system had worked great up to this point, but we suddenly found ourselves with a wonderful llama who had come down with a mysterious illness. Moche's head hung lower, his big black eyes no longer sparkled, and he didn't seem to be eating much. Nothing the vet had done seemed to help. Melissa loved Moche deeply, and wore an almost constant frown as she worried about how to help him. She tried all sorts of medications. She paid a vet who specialized in llamas to travel two hours to check him out. No one seemed to really know what was wrong with him. No one knew how to help.

He didn't seem in immediate danger, but something just wasn't right. All we could do was plod through our days as usual, but both of us found our gaze turning often toward his pen, watching for any change. Melissa wore down, caring for Moche, for her mother, for the farm, and dealing with my anxieties. I continued to dream of drowning, of becoming a mermaid, and of swimming away from the chaos.

ducks and tattoos

not content with just chickens and those blasted geese, Melissa wanted ducks. That was all we needed—more animals to care for. By this point in our farming career, I'd become, shall we say, a bit edgy? No, let's say overloaded, totally overwhelmed. I dreamt of the good old days when all we'd had to care for were two dogs and a twenty by twenty townhouse backyard. Therefore Melissa approached the subject of ducks cautiously.

"Ducks are beautiful," she said. "They're really cute and funny. You'll like them."

"No."

"They're so soft, and we can sell them for meat when they're old enough."

"If you get ducks, then I get a tattoo."

"What?"

"A tattoo."

"You want a what?"

"It's not such a big deal. Lots of women get them."

She tugged impatiently on the bill of her cap. "Well, this is a surprise. I suppose next you'll be buying a Harley."

"I married a farmer, you married a biker babe."

She grimaced. "A tattoo's more expensive than a few ducks."

"And requires no care whatsoever."

Melissa sighed. "Okay, it's deal. If I get ducks, then you get a tattoo." Neither of us believed the other would happen. Exactly three days later a friend called. Her uncle had "rescued" fifteen baby ducks from the state fair. Did we want them?

Melissa said yes, and I started calling tattoo shops to get their rates. I had no idea what design I would want to permanently affix to my body, so began considering all the possibilities. A discrete rose? A butterfly? An animal? An abstract design? It finally hit me that once it was on my body, it couldn't come off. This was a stupid idea, but I couldn't shake the determined voice that yearned for a tattoo. However, I needed a design that had enough meaning I could live with it for the rest of my life. As a teenager I had collected unicorns; after only a few years I was sick of the pastel, dreamy beasts. If I'd gotten a unicorn tattoo, that fad would have haunted me forever. My next fixation had been owls, after a tiny screech owl had perched on my tent several nights running as I camped in northern California. What if I'd gotten an owl tattoo? This is why teens shouldn't get tattoos—bodies would become shrines to all our short-lived obsessions as we aged. I put the tattoo idea on hold. Besides, I had nothing to celebrate yet, no transforming event to observe with a tattoo.

The baby ducks came, and were cute for about a week, with their soft down, squishy chests, tiny webbed feet, and smooth, petite bills. The tiny yellow and brown fuzzies quickly matured into white and brown ducks. In a few months the females would lay an egg a day, then walk away. They had absolutely no interest in interrupting their busy lives to sit on eggs for four weeks to hatch ducklings. Why sit around in a boring nest box with a bunch of broody hens when you could be marching around the farm single file, quacking raucously for no apparent reason?

So Melissa gathered the duck eggs and slipped them under the chicken hens who had gone broody. For weeks, all a broody hen wants to do is sit there, warming her eggs, staring off into space while the fertilized egg beneath her develops. Whatever hatched beneath her, the hen accepted as her own. This made for astonishingly diverse family groups roaming the yard, like the white hen with three speckled brown chicks, two yellow ducklings and two black and yellow ducklings. Melissa created multicultural family after family.

When an inattentive baby lost sight of Mom, the chick or duckling would stand still and peep or quack as loudly as it could. Those tiny peeps of fear could reach me in every room of the house, so I grew accustomed to putting down my pen, pulling on my boots, and letting the insistent peeping lead me to the lost baby. Oddly enough, the baby ducks were a welcome way to escape my miserable attempts to write. They gave me a break from hours of dealing with student assignments (which, thankfully, had nothing to do with ducks themselves.) I'd chase the baby, corner it, scoop it up in my hands, and track down its mother. The baby would scoot toward the clucking hen, quacking indignantly about the giant who'd attacked her, then immediately start exploring again, the very thing that had gotten it lost in the first place.

The ducklings were so new, so curious, so energized by life. Hmm. Perhaps a duck tattoo?

Nah.

small losses

Living in Minnesota means that you only have about five months to grow and enjoy flowers, and as fall deepens, you hope for continued warm weather so your flowers won't freeze. But cold isn't the only danger for flowers.

One fall afternoon Melissa called me to the front door and pointed to the tall flower box enclosing our well cap. "Look! Aren't they cute?" Four adolescent ducks were lined up one beside the other, eating my red and pink moss roses that were just at head-height. I shrieked and ran outside, flapping my arms and cussing out those four "cute" ducks. My control over my flowers went downhill from there. They discovered the marigolds in the flower boxes by the house, and there was nothing I could do unless I spent all day outside guarding the only spots of color in our yard.

That's when I patted the cement on the front step next to me and asked Melissa to sit down for a minute. "Help me out here," I said. "There seem to be an unreasonable amount of poultry patrolling the place. What's going on? I thought we were going to hatch a few batches then stop."

Melissa just shrugged. "I'm not sure," she said without looking me in the eye.

"How come it's September and there are still new babies running around?"

Melissa's head dropped. She took off her cap, scratched her head, then tugged the cap back in place. "I've been . . . well, I've been putting eggs under broody hens all summer."

"Not just a few batches in the spring?"

"No. I couldn't stop. The babies are so cute, and when they start pecking their way out of their shells, it's just so amazing. . . ."

"You have a problem, you know."

"I know."

"Next year—"

"I'll only raise a few batches, I promise." There were no organizations for people addicted to poultry, so I had my doubts.

Every morning we fed the chickens, gave them fresh water, then opened the chicken door. They were free to roam as far as they wanted, eating grass and bugs and kitchen scraps. The ducks established their independence by roaming the farthest and the longest. As dusk approached, Serge headed for the shed, Sonny and the other chickens returned to the chicken room for the night, and the ducks partied outside. We could hear them quacking in the dark up by the hay bales, then in the ram pen, then, more wild quacking as they slowly wandered back toward the chicken room.

Chickens have short lives, too short in some cases. Early that fall, as Melissa and I stood in the driveway discussing a fencing project, I gasped, then pointed to an alarming pile of white feathers by the garden. Chickens sometimes rest by spreading out, sticking one leg straight out to the side, their heads and beaks always upright. But not that night.

We dashed over to the dead chicken. It was Serge. Melissa dropped to her knees as she moaned the rooster's name. We checked his body for signs that Sonny had attacked him; there were none, so Sonny would live to see another day. Serge's heart must have stopped. Melissa gathered the rooster's limp, still-warm body into her arms, and rocked quietly. The setting sun threw our shadows against the house, turning everything around us a warm gold.

Swallowing hard, I rested my hand on Melissa's bent head, but said nothing. I stroked Serge's neck and cape, amazed at his silky softness. Serge had not been the first chicken we'd lost, but losing him was the hardest.

Melissa's sadness only fueled my own and contributed to my downward spiral. Moche's health was still declining, and if it hurt this much to lose Serge, what would it feel like to lose Moche? I clearly wasn't cut out to be a farmer. I wasn't cut out to be a writer either. What the hell was I going to do with my life?

lesbians and straight lines

i had no time or energy to answer deep, searching life questions because fencing filled my days. Building fences was usually a two-person job. We spent hours building three-wire fences to break the pastures into paddocks. We could handle this type of job, for it only required a hammer to pound in the slender fiberglass posts and a post pounder for steel posts.

We needed a small fence around about an acre of land near the house. Melissa was busy with other farm projects, so I took on this fence myself.

I paced off the fence line, aiming for four lines to form a solid rectangle. I pounded a post, moved twenty feet, pounded another. Once I pounded the posts, I stepped back, looked down each line, and grimaced. I hadn't built fence lines, I'd built four slalom runs with clever, tight zigzags. Tough. I wasn't going to pull out all those posts and do it again. Perfectionism had never been my particular burden.

We then asked the company who'd built the perimeter in the south part of the farm to return and fence in the north twenty acres. They pounded posts, strung wire, and installed a wide red hollow tube gate. To use this twenty acres in our pasture rotation system, all we had to do was install the three-wire fences that broke the huge acreage into runs. Imagine the pasture as a huge loaf of bread which needed to be sliced into ten pieces, each 140 feet wide. This measurement was critical. If the runs were 140 feet apart, then the Electronet, which was 150 feet long, would easily reach from run to run. If the runs were more than 150 apart, the Electronet wouldn't reach.

We mapped it out. There would be nine fences running parallel to each other. Each fence would run for approximately 750 feet, so we faced the daunting task of building over 6,750 feet of fence. Time for a party.

We sent out invitations to all our friends, and ten crazies agreed to show up, anxious to flee the city, even if it meant tackling fencing, something few of them had done. Before they came, however, Melissa and I got everything ready. We started with our backs next to the perimeter fence, which was straight, then paced off 140 feet and put down a florescent orange flag. We returned to the perimeter fence and did the same thing twelve more times until we had a lovely row of orange flags flapping in the wind. This would be fence number one.

From this row of flags, we paced off another 140 feet and put down a flag. This would be fence number two. It took us hours and hours to walk the entire twenty acres, measuring and remeasuring, but finally all nine fence lines were marked with flags.

Fencing day went great. Some friends forced tight, spring-loaded wire guides onto the slender fiberglass posts. Others strung three wires on the ground along the flagged fence lines. Others constructed wire doohickeys that would connect the wire to the end posts. Others pounded in the fiberglass posts. Others strung the wire. We laughed and talked, and inhaled the cream of broccoli soup and homemade bread a friend brought.

The party had to break up late afternoon before we could finish all the fences, but most were done or in progress. The next morning Melissa and I stood on the top of the hill, marveling at what our friends had helped us create. Morning dew clung to the wires, so it seemed the pasture was strung with sparkling parallel spider webs.

In a few days, we prepared to move the sheep for the first time onto this twenty-acre pasture. Melissa set up the first Electronet, the 150-foot net that would run from fence line to fence line, breaking up the long runs into smaller paddocks. But the run was wider than 150 feet. She ran out of net before she reached the fence, which meant the Electronet was useless.

She came back to the house to get me, and we rushed back together. The two fence lines were too far apart! We scooped up the net fence and tried another spot. The Electronet didn't reach there either. This was a disaster.

The first thing we did was jump up and down and yell at each other. Yet another fight. But we quickly stopped when we remembered we'd laid out the fence lines together. Anger turned to horror and we collapsed on the pasture, laying back to watch disgustingly cheerful clouds drift overhead. Cars passed on the highway nearby, taking happy carefree people to fun and exciting destinations, while we faced the horrible truth.

"Fence number one isn't straight," I whispered.

"I know." Horror settled deep into our bones. It wasn't straight because our clever line of orange flags hadn't been straight.

"That means . . ." I could go no farther.

Melissa sighed. "None of the fences are straight." Because we'd used the first fence line as our guide, the remaining eight fences would form that same slanted angle.

We had no choice but to pull out every post, move every wire, and straighten out each fence, a huge task we had to stack on top of our already-full schedule. What was it with lesbians and straight lines?

nature's sentimental journey

as that year progressed, I began to notice nature poetry everywhere I turned—in the local newspaper, the *Minnesota Monthly,* on the radio, in books and magazines. I developed an unreasonable dislike for those giddy poems and essays that described an author's appreciation for nature. The writers twittered on about the birds at their feeders, the morning dew, the breeze softly blowing through the wildflowers, about their connection to and respect for the earth, about their deeply personal and spiritually moving encounters with nature. Help, I wanted to scream. What about the *rest* of the story? What about what *really* happened in nature?

I foamed at the mouth for awhile, feeling too unfriendly to appreciate beauty. Was I just so cranky about being stuck on this farm that I couldn't enjoy the world around me? I started to feel like a Poetry Scrooge, unwilling to give out even a penny's worth of praise for either prose or poetry writing. But with much nature writing, it felt as if the writers weren't really seeing nature, but simply romanticizing what they thought they saw, throwing up walls to keep out the ugly. After months on the farm, I'd come to see that nature had an underbelly, something you couldn't observe on a fifteen-minute nature walk. Living in the country means sharing your world with the wild creatures around you—they see more of your lives, you see more of theirs.

The part of nature that no one talks about is death. Our cat Oliver, a white and orange stray who adopted us, would drop off dead ground squirrels as an offering to the family meal. A hen would suddenly die, legs stiff, feathers matted, eyes covered with pale, pebbly eyelids. A nocturnal raccoon, sick with distemper or rabies, staggered down the road in broad daylight so Melissa shot it, both to put it out of its misery and to save other animals from being infected.

When cars and nature intersect, the results are often devastating for nature, yet how many people write poems about road kill? On my daily walks down our quiet, dead-end gravel road, I found a small toad squashed by a car, a slender red-bellied snake cut in half, a baby wild turkey dead on its side, feathers lifting slightly in the morning breeze.

Cranky now, I plotted Alternative Nature Poems, revolutionary works I would write were I a poet, which, happily, I was not. Instead of writing about the great horned owl flying through the night, I *could* write about the glistening strands of rabbit intestine the owl left draped across the birdhouse roof the next morning. They looked almost iridescent blue in the sunshine, and were all that was left of the rabbit, save three clumps of fur on the ground, and one stuck on the rough cedar birdhouse. I stood there, struggling with sadness for the rabbit, and joy that the owl's young had food in their bellies.

How many poets have written of that chance encounter with a deer in the woods, where the human and deer stand still as stone as they contemplate one another? They write of the connection they feel, the thrill of being so near a wild animal. No, if I were to write a poem about deer, I would write about the dead fawn Melissa and I found while exploring the thicket near our creek:

small, reddish brown, perfect black nose and long black lashes, curled up in the lush green grass as if she were asleep. Melissa checked her hooves—the tiny membranes across their tips were still intact, so the fawn had never stood. The doe had cleaned her off, probably nudging her, trying to get her to stand, but the fawn had only curled up and died. When Melissa took my dad there the next day, the fawn's body was gone, dragged off by a coyote or a skunk who would chew on the perfect fawn and leave the skin and bones to rot and sink into the earth. Nature persists by consuming itself.

I could write a poem about the majestic llama standing on the hillside, surveying his flock. To reveal nature's underbelly, however, I'd also have to add the squeaking. When I moved Moche and the sheep to a new paddock, five minutes later I heard this high-pitched, terrified squeaking coming from near Moche, who stood still, unconcerned. Confused, wondering how this huge beast could be making this sound, I walked closer. The squeaking grew weaker. That's when I figured out the noise came from *under* Moche's front right hoof. Some poor mouse had been going about his day when a three-hundred-pound llama with broad camel feet stepped on him, and didn't feel like moving.

Or I could write about the day Melissa and I went snowshoeing with some friends by our creek on a sunny, crisp January morning. I was the first to reach the pristine snow beyond the gate, and the first to find the marks of hawk wings brushing across the snow. The fresh snow had recorded each feather tip on the wide wings. Ten inches from this beauty, however, was a depression in the snow, about a foot across, that was lined with the soft underfeathers of a female pheasant. The four of us stood around the scene, recreating it. Hawk brushes snow as he slows his descent. Talons grab the pheasant. Brief struggle. Hawk lifts off and flies away with his now wounded meal.

Writing about only the lovely side of nature, or the romantic side of farming, or the joys of country living, feels disrespectful. Nature is not some pristine concept to be marveled at or worshiped through a glass display case. We are part of nature, not just observers, and must acknowledge that nature has winners and losers, predators and prey.

This, I see now, was a shift I had made since my time on the farm. Death was no longer an abstract concept, but a dead lamb and a dead chicken and a dead raccoon and a dead fawn. I'd been spending time with farmers, who didn't like death any more than I did, but who took it in stride, who recognized it as just part of their day. There were no fences high enough or strong enough to keep out death.

I have come to see that all I can do, out of respect, is pay *attention* to nature, to see it for what it is, not for what I want it to be. I considered this as I stared at the wing prints in the light snow, at the soft pheasant feathers. Yes, it is true, as many poets have so appropriately captured, that nature could be beautiful. But just as often nature could be brutal. Now and then, if I really paid attention, I found something that was both.

—◦◦◦—

BUT HERE I was, only several years into farming, and I was tired of paying attention. I was tired of learning the harsh realities of nature. I was tired of being tired. I was tired of living someone else's dream.

the tattoo of transformation, sort of . . .

more loss

life on a farm rolls on relentlessly, with no regard for whether you've had too many hard days in a row and need a break, or whether you're sick or depressed or upset about the latest presidential election, or whether your father (or father-in-law) has died. Losing a family member doesn't prepare you for losing livestock. Losing livestock doesn't prepare you for losing a family member.

Farming losses tend to pile up like a multiple-car highway accident in thick fog. Those losses may be separated by a few weeks, or a few years, but they all contribute to the same fatalistic acceptance of this hard fact: when your farm is teeming with animal life, it's only a matter of time before some of those lives end. Death happens. As many cynical farmers put it, "Where there's livestock, there's also dead stock."

Sheep tend to keep their illnesses to themselves, so it's only when they're nearly dead that an observant shepherd can even tell they're sick. If a lamb stands hunched over with a glazed expression, but races away in terror when you approach, you might have a chance of saving her . . . if you can catch her.

If a lamb doesn't run when you approach, your chances of saving her are slim, but you have to try. If a lamb doesn't run, then doesn't struggle when you pick her up and strap her into the basket on your four-wheeler and drive her back to the barn, she'll likely be dead within the hour. What killed her? Probably an intestinal worm that consumed so much of the lamb's blood that she became anemic and died. All pasture-based systems struggle with this problem—as animals graze, they ingest the eggs and larvae of worms attached to the blades of grass. A vigilant shepherd will "worm" her sheep, or administer a hefty dose of wormer, throughout the summer. Doing this is like trying to administer a dose of castor oil to a reluctant child, but the wormer flushes the worms from the animal's system. Despite this, some animals die anyway.

———

FALL ARRIVED, AND I was still on the farm. Twice now, I'd looked for apartments in the paper for Tory and me. Twice I'd failed. Twice I'd nearly opened my mouth during a fight to shout, "That's it. I'm leaving!" But I didn't. Chicken. A total chicken.

Tory loved fall, and so I'd take her on short walks down the driveway. Anything farther strained her hips. Despite her pain, she kept to her old habits, the most irritating of which was stealing shoes. She didn't chew them, she just stole them and stashed them under the big desk.

We gave her cosequin, a drug that builds up a cartilage-like material around the joints, and thought we saw a small difference. She spent more time outside, wandering farther and longer. Sometimes she was gone for thirty minutes, and was wet and breathless when she returned, tongue hanging out but happy. Twice she came home with her long ears so full of burrs they stuck straight out from her head like Pippi Longstocking's braids. Melissa patiently combed them all out.

A few times she even grabbed a stick and ran toward me as she used to, head shaking, daring me to try to take it away. She used to win our tug-of-war games when her hips worked.

One night, as Melissa and I returned from a birthday party, I unlocked the front door and Amber and Robin bolted past me. I knew Tory was in the bedroom, but she didn't respond to my call. I turned on the bedroom light and froze at the sight of Tory's huge, unblinking eyes, her swollen tongue. She jerked once and we ran to her, crying out, rubbing her, rolling her, trying to call back her life. I felt rapid-fire beating under my hand rocking her chest, then nothing.

As I bent over Tory's lifeless body, it felt as if my ribs were breaking. I stroked her ears and kissed her long brown nose. Half an hour later, I wrapped her up in a large towel and Melissa carried her limp bulk out to the pickup. I cradled her head, fanning her long ears out across my arm, while Melissa drove us to the vet clinic. Before the vet put her body into the cooler, I snipped off a lock of her silky hair.

The next day Melissa and I walked through the house, gathering up the shoes Tory had stashed. "Here's my black sneaker, and my brown sandal," I said.

"I can't find one of my old sneakers, the ones I wear to paint," Melissa said.

We looked again, but still couldn't find it, so I decided Tory took it with her.

⸻

AMBROSIA HAD PROVED to be a marvelous goat, calm and gentle with children, an excellent mother to her kids, and a willing surrogate mother to bottle lambs in the late spring. We kept one of her babies, named her Betsy, and had high hopes she would follow in her mother's footsteps.

One frigid January afternoon Melissa stopped into the barn to check on things. Ambrosia was standing by the big door, seemingly fine, but when Melissa returned thirty minutes later, Ambrosia had begun trembling and grinding her teeth. Melissa took her temperature. We gave her a few medications we had on hand, but we didn't know what was wrong with her. Within minutes, she dropped to her knees, trembling violently now, her vision glazed and unblinking, then fell over on her side. Melissa ran for the phone while I knelt by Ambrosia's side, the cold weather forgotten as I draped myself over the convulsing goat, praying that she was not in too much pain, whatever was coursing through her body.

The vet came quickly, but before he could really get the IV going and do much, Ambrosia stopped convulsing and died in Melissa's arms. We stared in shock, Melissa rocking the 150-pound goat gently. "Ambrosia, Ambrosia, don't go." No response. Within thirty minutes she'd gone from a healthy animal to a dead one.

As the vet quietly packed up his equipment, Melissa and I struggled for control, hanging on until the vet's taillights disappeared around the curve in the driveway. I don't remember much of that night—we spent it crying, and wondering what we could have done differently. Had there been signs of something we'd missed? Would another drug have helped? Why had she convulsed so violently?

The next morning Melissa did what she did best—take action. We'd recently met a woman who worked for the Minnesota Science Museum, and she'd told us the museum had an extensive collection of animal skeletons that scientists across the country came to study. Melissa called Jackie and asked her if the museum needed a goat skeleton.

Jackie practically yelped with excitement. Just the day before the museum employees had been discussing an upcoming exhibit of Catalhöyük, an excavation in Turkey, one of the first places man ceased his wandering and settled into a city. The Science Museum needed to entirely recreate the dig because the Turkish officials wouldn't let them remove anything from the country. The museum had almost everything it needed, except goat bones.

That very day Jackie braved the icy roads to drive down for Ambrosia's body. It took four of us, but using a plastic sled, we hoisted our beloved goat into the back of Jackie's pickup. Melissa and I were oddly comforted—at least Ambrosia's death could benefit someone.

Melissa's only request of Jackie's boss was that, after they examined Ambrosia's body, they let us know if they found anything to help us understand why she'd died. Two days later the call came. Ambrosia died of a massive aneurism in her brain. There was absolutely nothing we could have done to save her, or the three babies she carried.

A few months later we visited the Science Museum, and spoke with Jackie. When I mentioned we were going to attend the laser show, she gave us both a funny look, then took a deep breath. "You need to know, then, that in the hallway you take to the laser theater, you'll pass a large window into one of the science labs. In that window we have a working display showing how insects help us clean dead flesh off the skeletons we keep here."

Melissa figured it out first. "Ambrosia."

Jackie nodded.

As we entered the hallway and passed the large window into the brightly lit lab, I focused on my shoes and did not stop until I reached the theater. Melissa, ever the scientist, stopped. She could tell it was Ambrosia by the hooves—they had needed trimming before she'd died, and they still did. A few signs in the window explained the process, and Melissa felt the whole exhibit was well done—educational and interesting.

We were still heartbroken over Ambrosia, but at the same time filled with pride that she was teaching people even in her death.

———

MOST OF THE snow had melted, and leaves were beginning to appear on a few trees. The grapevines were coming to life as the buds began to swell, and the Midwest began losing that ugly brown-gray look it suffered between snowmelt and true spring.

But as the weather warmed and the farm came to life, Moche continued to deteriorate. Melissa had tried everything. One vet thought perhaps his rumen wasn't working correctly, so he wasn't getting enough to eat. His face had begun to sink in like an old man's. For weeks Melissa gave him Probios, a thick blue paste meant to jump-start his rumen. No change.

Another vet thought it might be a meningeal worm. This is a nasty bug that lives in the brain lining of deer, a host not bothered by the worm. But when the worm makes its way into other mammals, the results are not as benign. The unwilling host's body begins putting up a fight, shutting down systems in the body until the animal can't walk. Several times Moche had fallen, and could not get up without our help. We tried treating him for this, but no improvement.

Eventually Melissa was spending over an hour a day just with Moche, encouraging him to eat grain out of her hand, leading him to the water trough trying to get him to drink. But more and more, it just felt like no one was home, and that he was just going through the motions for Melissa's sake, not his own.

Early May, just days before the lambs would arrive, I trudged up to the barn to check on Moche. I could see a golden mound of hair in the shadows of the barn, so I slammed the gate loudly behind me. That would be enough to wake Moche so he'd lift his head and gaze at me with those black liquid eyes. But the mound didn't move, because Moche had died during the night. I stood over his body, too stunned to cry, willing him to get to his feet in that ungainly llama fashion. Didn't happen, of course, so I dragged myself down to the house to break the news to Melissa.

She had spent months trying to nurse Moche through his mysterious illness, and her deep sadness was matched only by her sense of failure. By spending so much time with him, she'd developed a bond that was painfully ripped apart at Moche's death. After he had died, Melissa spent over an hour alone with Moche in the barn, talking with him and trying to come to terms with her grief. She clipped some of his long, curly wool as a keepsake, and removed his green halter.

In the middle of our sorrow, we had two practical problems to address. What does one do with the dead body of a three-hundred-pound animal? We had no way of moving him out of the barn. After a few days, we contacted Paul, our original sheep mentor, and he came over immediately with his skid-loader, gently scooped up Moche's body, and deposited him in a pit we'd had dug several years before, one we used specifically to dispose of dead livestock. Paul put him on one side and covered the body with several loads of soil. The Science Museum wanted Moche's skeleton, but decided to let it sit in the ground for a few years.

The second practical problem was that we were expecting almost one hundred baby lambs to be born in the next few weeks, with coyotes hovering nearby, and we had no llama. We returned to the woman who'd sold us Moche, and she took us out into a paddock filled with fifteen male llamas. All fifteen came running when we appeared, their ears perked in alarm at this intrusion. The llamas ended up circling us, fifteen inquisitive guys concerned about our presence. But as we stood talking, one by one the llamas began to relax and wander away, grazing on lush grass at the far end of the pasture. Finally only one llama remained, a dark brown beauty with a white chest and head. His ears were still perked forward, and he remained vigilant, clearly uncomfortable we were still invading his territory.

Melissa and I looked at each other. "We'll take him."

The woman delivered him the next week, and we named him Chachi. He was even more aloof than Moche, but bonded quickly with the sheep. One of the first nights, when dusk fell and a light-bulb still burned in the barn, shooting an unnaturally bright light out the barn door, Chachi was so alarmed that he gave a wild, trumpeting cry and bunched the sheep into a tight circle around him. While he could never totally replace Moche, we quickly learned Chachi had a style all his own.

Every time we lost an animal, my thoughts seemed to flicker over the other major losses in my life—my grandparents years ago, Melissa's father, my parents' marriage, and oh—what was that activity I used to do? Something that involved a pen and paper and lots of words.

shadowboxing

my size 7 underwear still resided in the same drawer with Melissa's ridiculously petite 5s, but would my life improve if those size 7s found their way to another drawer in another dresser in a new place of my own, one that didn't have duck shit on the front step? Leaving the farm was certainly an option. Who could blame me? Picking placenta out of one's hair, or finding bits of hay in one's underwear, or digging sheep manure out from under one's fingernails certainly isn't for everyone.

I was afraid to tell Melissa I was considering leaving her. None of our friends knew what was going on; we were great at hiding our struggles. Besides, even if they'd known, I wouldn't have put them in the awkward position of having to take sides.

I finally suggested counseling. Hey, I was about two more fights away from leaving, so what could it hurt? Melissa agreed we could see a therapist. As we drove to the Twin Cities, my hopes soared. Maybe Barbara could help us stop fighting. Maybe she could prescribe a pill to help me farm. Valium came to mind.

We settled into her two overstuffed chairs and began. The point of the counseling session was to focus on our relationship, but ten minutes into the session, all we'd talked about was Melissa's anger toward the world. Thirty minutes passed and Barbara was still addressing most of her questions to Melissa. Every attempt I made to steer the conversation toward us failed. I sank lower into my chair and gave up. Melissa talked and talked. She admitted she was tired of the conflict raging within her; she was constantly arguing with people in her head, always ready for a fight.

Finally the therapist revealed her concerns. "You have all the symptoms of a brain chemistry problem."

"You mean I'm depressed?"

"No. Your brain chemistry might have changed in the last few years. If your serotonin levels are too low, this could cause your mood swings, explosive anger, and paranoia." Until Melissa dealt with this problem, it made no sense to work on the relationship. She encouraged Melissa to see her physician to discuss seratonin replacement therapies.

Melissa winced at the idea. She'd taken antidepressants in her early twenties and found they did nothing except add twenty pounds. "I don't know," she said. "Things have to be pretty bad to take those drugs."

I cleared my throat. "I've almost left you this summer—twice."

Her body stiffened, her eyes widened. "Really?" she whispered. "Jesus." She dropped her head.

Barbara outlined the new seratonin replacement drugs, explaining they were more effective, more specific than the drugs of twenty years ago. We thanked her, hugged her, then left.

This was one decision Melissa had to make on her own. We talked for hours, or rather she talked and I listened. She'd learned to live with headaches, but this rage, the constant bickering in her head, her self-image as Dr. Jekyll/Ms. Hyde, was too much to bear any longer. Finally she decided to give the drugs a try, not just to save our relationship, but to seek relief.

Melissa took her first little yellow pill one night before bed.

The next morning I woke up, rolled over, and discovered Melissa awake, staring at the ceiling.

"What's up?" I asked.

"I'm singing."

"You're just laying there quietly."

"No," she said. "In my head. I'm singing."

"No fights?"

"None. I'm just singing."

We fell silent. Could just one pill be that powerful?

That day Melissa stood at the sink washing dishes, and started crying. "Do other people have this quiet, calm in their heads?" she finally was able to ask.

"Yes." My anxiety aside, things in my head were fairly quiet.

That winter we continued working to finish the basement, spraying texture on the walls, painting, installing a drop ceiling, selecting a laminate floor for my office. Finally my room was done enough I could move in. Of course, since I no longer wrote, I didn't need an office, but Melissa and I both pretended I did.

As we worked I watched Melissa for alarming changes. Was her personality abnormal, different? Was she falsely happy? No, she continued to be Melissa, but an earlier one, the one I'd lived with until just a few years ago. Her anger eased. Instead of erupting, she could stop, clearly state why she was upset, and suggest ways to resolve it.

But a funny thing happened. I'd learned how to fight with her these last few years, but now I ended up just shadowboxing. Two weeks after Melissa had started on medication, she came in one morning from chores. "Honey, next time you feed the goats, could you make sure you latch the gate? They—"

"What? I've done something wrong again?" I shouted. "I'm always doing something wrong, aren't I?"

"No, it's just that—"

"I'm so sick of being yelled at," I yelled. "Why can't you stop yelling at me?"

"I'm not yelling at you." Her voice was even.

"Yes, you are. You're yelling at me!"

"No, I'm not." I stopped. No, she wasn't. "Cath, you're the one who's yelling. I just want to talk to you."

"Oh . . . okay . . . sorry."

As I struggled to stop fighting with Melissa, it suddenly seemed important to give us another chance. Over the winter life continued to improve. When I thought about leaving, it made me sad. No Melissa, no Robin the border collie, no baby ducks peeping, no bottle lambs to feed and cuddle.

I spent the winter working, carving out more time to write, visiting family and friends, putting jigsaw puzzles together with Melissa, and reading in my chair near the wood stove.

There wasn't one moment when I knew I would stay, but lots of unremarkable moments that passed without notice. Winter was a quiet time on the farm, so with the chaos stripped away, I could see and appreciate the bare bones of our relationship. Those bones were sturdy, healthy, and strong enough to withstand stress.

By spring, I had made a tentative truce with my favorite member of my cozy little ménage à trois. I didn't want to leave her. I still loved her. She cracked me up nearly every day, and she adored me and wanted me to write and be happy.

Of course, lambs were only days away by now, so once again the largest member of the ménage à trois would crap on my creativity and zap my energy. Threesomes were a messy, messy business, and somehow, I had to figure out how to deal with that.

i build a fence

life definitely improved. Melissa and I talked more. We fought less. But farm life was still chaotic—we were still learning, still building fences, still laying water lines throughout the pastures, still struggling with weeds in the vineyard.

I survived another lambing season. Melissa was becoming an old pro, now able to step back and let the ewe do most of the work. She no longer worried about when to intervene, for she knew if the lamb hadn't come on its own after a few hours, it needed help. I had even progressed to the proud point that, while holding down a ewe as Melissa delivered the lamb, I no longer sobbed into the ewe's neck. Now I just moaned. We both agreed there was hope for me.

We had over one hundred lambs born. After a few weeks, the pasture looked like an out-of-control daycare, with white, black, and speckled babies everywhere. Damn, but they were cute, with their oversized windmill ears, tiny noses, and bellies round with milk. And since we'd figured out that ram lambs would grow faster if we didn't castrate them, we tried something new we'd read about, turning ram lambs into crypt orchids—sterile but intact males. If you pushed the testicles up into the lamb's body, then banded the scrotum, the animal was still technically intact, so would grow quickly, but the heat of the animal's body would kill the sperm in the testicles, rendering the little guy sterile. That way the ram lambs could continue to live with the ewes without us fearing any unauthorized sheep sex. Damn, we were clever.

We were both getting better at this. The farm was up and running, and Melissa had turned into an amazing veterinarian, electrician, fencer, engineer, carpenter, and farm manager. As we began to feel sort of comfortable with this life as farmers, a tiny thought formed in my head. I let it sit quietly in the dark for a few weeks to see if it would take root. It did. Yes, yes, yes. This was brilliant. This was the answer. If there had been a book called *Problem Solving for Dummies*, this solution would have been on the first page.

I finally gave voice to my idea one post-lambing day as we sat on our "porch" swing, each munching on our second Fudgesicle of the morning, and I had just loosened my jeans, wondering why, with all this farm work, I was putting on weight, not taking it off.

Spring in Minnesota is energizing, with birds busily building nests, baby lambs and goats scampering on the heels of their mothers, a hint of warmth on the breeze, and bright, almost Crayola-green grass. Melissa and I swung in companionable silence, then the words popped out of my mouth, sudden as a burp.

"I can't help with the farm anymore."

Busy licking off her stick, and wondering if she should go for thirds, Melissa didn't hear me, so I repeated myself.

"What? Sell the farm?"

"No. You farm. I write. I don't do chores. I don't help unless you absolutely need me to help. And I mean *need* me, not *want* me to help." There. I'd said it. In front of God, the chickens, the ducks, the goats, Melissa, everybody.

Robin raced back and forth in front of us, shaking a stick to kill it dead. The goats basked on the top of their electrical spools, chewing their cud. Melissa cleared her throat. "I do all the farm work."

"Yes." Suddenly everything felt right. "I only help when there's an emergency. I only help when there are two-people projects, and then we agree to a time."

"I need another Fudgesicle."

We ate and swung for a few more minutes. She licked off yet another empty Fudgesicle stick. "You'd be happier that way, wouldn't you?"

"I have to get back to what I love. We've gotten the farm up and running. Our learning curve has flattened out. If I don't put up a fence between me and the farm, I'll lose myself entirely. I've already lost so much that I don't know if I can get it back. But I have to try." Boundaries, boundaries, boundaries. I needed them desperately. Besides, I didn't need to Google "couples running a business together" to see the truth: life in a small business might work better if there was only one boss. Managing by consensus, or by my anxiety, certainly wasn't working well. It was clearly time to rely on that old canoeing metaphor Melissa had come up with years ago. When it came to the farm, Melissa would be Captain Kirk, and I would be the reliable, unflappable, anxiety-free Mr. Spock. Okay, at least I would be the reliable Mr. Spock.

By the time we'd emptied the Fudgesicle box, we'd agreed. Melissa would farm. I would write and work at my "off-farm" job of teaching writing through the correspondence course.

I wonder if Siamese twins undergo any sort of separation anxiety after surgery to disconnect them. My days began to take on a comforting structure, as I spent most of them in my office with the door closed. But I could feel Melissa moving about the farm as clearly as if we were joined at the hip. The first few months were hard. Melissa felt abandoned, as well she should. I felt guilty and defensive at the same time, frantic to protect my new life, even though nothing much was happening in my office.

We developed an irritating pattern. Melissa would come into the house, walk down the stairs, then stop before my closed door. We'd listen to each other breathe, Melissa wondering if her problem was worth bothering me, me wondering if her problem was worth bothering me. Most of the time she'd give a small sigh, then climb back up the stairs and out the door.

Too bad I couldn't leave it at that. I'd begin to worry. What did she need help with? Would she hurt herself if I didn't help? How were the animals? Was Chachi sick? Had Robin hurt himself? So I'd put down my pencil and head upstairs, looking out every window to see what she was up to. After wasting half an hour worrying, I'd trudge back downstairs.

Sometimes she knocked on my door and the poor thing met a fairly hostile writer. Unless an animal was bleeding to death, I maintained she shouldn't interrupt me. It didn't matter that when she knocked, I had been doing nothing but staring out my window and wondering what the hell to write about.

Soon she stopped coming downstairs, but would stop at the top of the stairs, reconsider, then leave. One afternoon after I heard this, I found myself leaping to my feet, bounding up the stairs, and running to the front door. "What did you want?" I called as she crossed the yard, ready to yell at her for almost-disturbing me.

She turned and shrugged. "Just wanted to tell you that I love you."

Oh.

Once I heard her outside my door, but she said nothing. While I had a door, I did not, as yet, have a doorknob. I looked up to find her staring at me through the round hole. It was such a funny sight I forgot to be angry.

Melissa began to learn her own limits. She learned how much, or how little, one person can do in a day. Tasks became more enjoyable for her because I wasn't there, pissing and moaning, bossing and criticizing and making both of us miserable.

Because she no longer had me to rely on for labor overflow, she had to plan ahead, think things through—in short, manage better. Ever since we had started the farm my sense of obligation and support kept me right there at her side to help, hands cupped to catch the water overflowing the bucket. Try doing anything else while your hands are filled with water.

By saying no, by removing myself as overflow, I broke free, and waited for something to shift in me. That fall and winter I still fled from the farm, but would occasionally offer to help. Together we fenced part of a paddock, and it went well. I didn't boss her around, and we didn't yell at each other once. I let go of whether our activity was the highest priority; this was Melissa's choice and somehow she got things done, even though it wasn't in the order I would have chosen.

Whenever Melissa and I walked through our pastures, Melissa occasionally dropped to her knees, reached into a thick patch of clover, and plucked a four-leaf clover. "How did you do that?" She would shrug, then ten minutes later find me another. "It's the pattern, I guess. I can see the shape of a four-leaf clover."

I always peered down as I walked, but could never see more than a dizzying mass of leaves. I even crouched before a specific patch, staring intently, searching for that elusive pattern she described. "Nothing here," I said. Melissa reached over my shoulder and pointed to one right under my nose.

Melissa tried to explain it to me. "You believe you'll find a rainbow after rain, so you look up, don't you? You know what to look for. If you believe you'll find four-leaf clovers, you look down and you'll find them." Soon she took to slipping the clovers into her wallet, presenting them to me as pressed works of art. "For you," she'd say.

I found red-bellied snakes. I found tiny toads and massive softball-sized toads. Once, walking through the pasture about ten steps ahead of Melissa, I even spotted a salamander, its black shiny skin dotted with yellow spots whose edges blurred like melted candle wax. For Melissa, salamanders brought back memories of mucking about in the neighborhood pond. Emboldened because I wore gloves, I scooped up the salamander and turned toward Melissa. She rewarded my sharp eye with a cry of delight.

But those blasted four-leaf clovers continued to elude. Then one morning we wormed the sheep for the third time in three months. Sweat pooled at the waistband of my jeans. My feet hurt. My arms ached, and we were only halfway through. I finally said, "I need a break." I dropped to the ground and leaned against a panel. Melissa joined me, exhausted as well.

I crossed my legs and leaned over my lap, now too tired to even sit up straight. I stared at the ground before me, thinking if I collapsed now maybe I'd never have to do this again. I moved the toe of my boot, and there it was. I froze, sure I was seeing things. But no, it was real. I plucked the four-leaf clover and turned to Melissa. "For you," I said.

ruby jumps over the fence

as the year progressed we both became more comfortable with the new arrangement. Melissa took pride in her ability to run things on her own. I took pride in my ability to spend all day in my office without writing anything worth the cost of the ink to print it. I continued to attend my two writing groups, and struggled to believe I could find my writing voice again. What did I have to write about? My life was pretty boring, my interests limited. What knowledge could I possibly share, what stories were inside me waiting to be born?

When the fuel company moved our diesel fuel tank from behind the shed to in front of it, they put the tank parallel to the shed. After a few months Melissa realized things would work better if the tank were rotated ninety degrees so she could get the tractor much closer to the tank's spigot.

"We can move this ourselves," she said, late that fall.

I stared up at the heavy steel tank, a massive rusty red cylinder about three feet in diameter, about six feet long, perched on a slender iron scaffolding about six feet high.

"No, we can't," I said. "It's nine feet tall. It's heavy."

"Yes, we can. It's nearly empty now."

"No, no, no."

"Yes, yes, yes." She marched into the shed and fired up the tractor. The tank would fall over and flatten us like pancakes. I just knew it. While things had been progressing well between us, Spock still struggled to trust the Captain's brash, can-do attitude.

Melissa positioned the tractor by the fuel tank, raised the loader up to the tank, then scampered up the hydraulic loader arms into the bucket. With my help from below, she wrapped heavy chains around the cylinder and attached them to two hooks welded onto the loader.

"So what's the plan?" I shouted over the tractor engine.

"I raise the loader, which lifts the tank off the ground." She waved her hands in the air. "It'll just hang there, so all you need to do is rotate it ninety degrees, then I'll lower it down. Easy as pie."

"Right," I said.

Melissa returned to the tractor seat, revved up the engine, then raised the loader as high as it would go. Unfortunately, that wasn't high enough. It lifted one end of the tank off the ground a few inches. The few gallons of fuel left inside sloshed to one end, upsetting the balance of the chains, and the whole tank began to tip. It stopped when one leg dug into the ground; the tank hung from the loader, doing a crazy, drunken pirouette. I tugged at the leg, trying to ignore the huge tank over my head, but scooted away when the chains slipped farther up the cylinder with a terrifying rasping clatter.

As I plastered myself against the shed, a curious calm spread over me. We were headed toward yet another disaster, yet the first thought that popped into my head wasn't an image of me crushed under the fuel tank, or of Melissa run over by a rolling fuel tank. My brain said, "Well, if you survive this, you can always write about it."

The fuel tank swung inches from my face as I wondered about karma and life lessons and why I was plastered against the shed with a fuel tank suspended before me. Why is it that those things we run away from always seem to follow us, unwilling to let go until we manage to learn something? My lesson, obviously, was to embrace the farm. But why? It didn't seem fair. Why couldn't my karmic lesson be to deal with life in a $500,000 beach house on the coast of California? God or the Universe or fate had nudged me onto this farm, so I might as well get on with it. "Bloom where you're planted," the t-shirt says.

Working together, we dislodged the fuel tank, raised it again, and set it down exactly where Melissa wanted it.

"Look at that," she said. "We did it."

"I knew we could," I replied, then squealed as Melissa chased me around the tractor.

That was it. I was ready to write about the farm. My friend Phyllis had sold a series of very short stories to Candlewick Press for their Brand New Reader series, and brought them to our writing group. She mentioned they were looking for more stories. Since each story only had to be eight sentences long, it seemed possible, something this nonwriter could do. As I drove home, possible ideas swirled through my head. What animal did I know more about than any other animal? Sheep. By the time I reached home, I had written eight stories in my head about a mischievous lamb named Ruby.

I sent them to the editor in charge of the series, and after I walked, slept, and ate on pins and needles for months, Candlewick bought them. For the first time, my writing and the farm mixed successfully.

One night I sat down and wrote about the day our tractor had died and Melissa had nearly been skewered by the neighbor's drag. I took it to my writing group and they laughed in all the right places. Then I wrote about the day I planted the two hundred grapevines upside down, and they laughed in all the right places. I gave a speech at Toastmasters about getting zapped by the electric fence, and they laughed in all the right places. I began to see that a life filled with mistakes was infinitely more amusing than a life without trouble. Eureka! An orderly life without woe was boring. Introduce a tractor, fifty sheep, two llamas (Melissa had purchased our second llama, Zipper, at a recent auction), and dozens of poultry into your life, and every day became pretty damned funny.

Except for the duck sex and Chachi's name. Those things weren't funny at all. One warm summer day I rested in the shade, finishing yet another Fudgesicle, when the two adult ducks decided to mate about four feet from me. Man, that can take a person's appetite away in no time.

As Mr. Duck finished and walked away, I noticed an alarming pink corkscrew of flesh hanging down from underneath him. My god, had his intestines ruptured or something? I hunted down Melissa, working in the shed, and asked about it.

"That's his penis. It always takes him a few minutes to draw it back up inside his body cavity."

"But it's shaped like a corkscrew." I didn't think that was funny at all.

Then came the day a college student friend was helping us in the vineyard lay more black mulch fabric. Chachi and Zipper watched from the pasture fifty feet away, glaring at this stranger who might want to harm their sheep. Zipper was a few years older than Chachi, all brown, a little tamer, and a little less vigilant, but he was working out fine.

After I told Heather the llamas' names, she sat back on her heels, a mischievous gleam in her eye. "Hmm, Zipper and Chachi?" She smiled. "Do you know what *chachi* means in Korean?"

Oh oh. "I'm not going to like this, am I?"

Her grin confirmed my prediction. "Remember that TV show *Happy Days* with the Chachi character?" I nodded. That had been partly where our llama's name had come from. "In Korea, *chachi* means 'penis.' The *Joanie Loves Chachi* show was very pop-ular there."

I snorted. Not funny. Not funny at all. God must have a pretty twisted sense of humor to stand by and watch two lesbians name their llamas Zipper and Penis.

back in the saddle again

not quite a year after my stunning announcement I would no longer participate in the farm, Melissa and I still struggled, but we were making progress. I was writing more, and had even started a novel for adults. I'd submitted an essay about farming to the *Writer's Digest* Annual Competition and won fourteenth out of thousands of entries. I discovered I wasn't as lazy as I'd thought, for now I had the energy to write. Yet something was still missing, something hadn't clicked into place. As I continued to push the farm away from me, it flowed right back at me.

One evening I watched one of my favorite movies, *The Hunt for Red October*. The submarine commander, played by Sean Connery, used a fascinating battle tactic: he turned his submarine *toward* the torpedo racing at him through the water. The sub and the torpedo met before the torpedo had armed itself, so it bounced harmlessly off the sub's hull.

Hey, what an idea. Why not move out to meet the farm, embracing it? I gave it a great deal of thought, then announced to Melissa I would do chores two days a week. She was skeptical, but willing and ready for a break. I chose Saturday and Sunday.

At first, Melissa would question me every time I returned. "Did you feed the chickens three scoops?"

"Yes."

"Did you remember to top off the rams' water?"

"Yes."

Weekend after weekend I trudged outside. I think Melissa expected me to tire and give up after just a week or two. She began to notice, however, that I didn't always do things exactly the way she did. We argued over method, but I insisted that if the end result was the same, why did I have to do things just like she did? I refused to be turned into a Melissa clone. At one point she literally stamped her foot, shouting, "You can't do chores anymore then."

That would have been the perfect opportunity to utter one simple word: "Okay." But my response surprised us both. "This is my farm, too, and I'm going to do chores." Chores got me outside. Chores strengthened my upper body. Chores made me feel part of the farm, but in a controlled way. Melissa was still responsible for large projects, for fixing things; I knew my contribution was small. But it was a contribution, and one I could build into my schedule, one I could control. I could then back off from the other farm duties with less guilt.

One of my chore days, a bright crisp March morning, about twenty degrees above zero, I fed the sheep, then noticed one girl off by herself, pawing at the ground. I chuckled, now expert enough to recognize she was mimicking the behavior of a ewe about to give birth. Cute. She must be responding to hormonal changes in her body, but she couldn't actually be in labor because our ewes weren't going to give birth for another two months, thanks to our tightly controlled approach to sheep sex. I watched her for a few minutes, then she turned her back to me. Oh. My. God. A water bag hung from her vulva, one of the first visible signs a sheep is in labor. No! It's March. It's cold. We only have a three-sided barn, which means we can't keep a baby warm. I ran to the house and yelled for Melissa.

By the time we got back up to the barn, a newborn lamb lay on the ground, steaming in the cool air.

We stared at the sight, unable to believe what our eyes were telling us. It was as if we'd seen a whale walking through our pasture. We looked at the ewe. We looked at each other. We looked at the rest of the flock. "Five months ago this ewe had unauthorized sheep sex," I said. Mid-October.

Melissa groaned. "The SEMSPA meeting. Remember?" Last fall we had hosted our shepherd group, and while touring the farm, we had all stood there watching a few ram lambs mounting the ewes. Melissa had explained about crypt orchids, and that the animals were sterile. Joe, our friend who'd been alarmed all those years ago to hear we were starting our flock with ewe lambs, winced. "You know, I've heard that sometimes that crypt orchid thing doesn't work, and the rams aren't sterile."

We had smiled and laughed, then forgot the whole thing, until now. We stared at the rest of the flock. How many more were on the verge of giving birth? Sick with fear, but determined to make this work, we started moving. Melissa and her sister Peg, who'd helped us shear, put the flock through the handling facility and felt the udders of all the sheep. Seventeen had udders full of milk, a sign they were due to give birth very soon. I set up pens inside the barn, lining them with straw bales and suspending a few heat lamps overhead. We stuck the seventeen in the pen nearest the barn so they could go inside when they gave birth.

For the next ten days we learned what it was like to lamb in the barn. We lost a lamb when the ewe gave birth outside in the cold. Whenever a lamb was born, we put the mother and lamb into a pen lined with straw. We turned on the heat lamps over the youngest babies. Unfortunately we forgot ewe number 66 was tall, so one morning the smell of burning wool greeted us as we approached the barn. The ewe had stood too long under the light, scorching her wool. Luckily it hadn't harmed her skin.

One morning Melissa found two lambs nearly dead from hypothermia and brought them back to the house. Watching over her shoulder, I shook my head. They were limp, unresponsive, beyond hope. But Melissa the Determined put colostrum into their bellies. She soaked them both in warm water, dried them, then put them on a heating pad and under a heat lamp.

Twenty-four hours later those two dead lambs were standing up in their box, crying for their mother. Melissa returned them to the barn, and the mom took them right away, nickering and using her nose to push them back toward her udder, encouraging them to nurse.

We had done it, and now had over thirty healthy lambs outside playing in the snow to prove it. Our confidence in ourselves, and in each other, jacked up many notches. We'd stayed relatively calm and focused, and had done what needed to be done.

I still feel flashes of pride that I was the one to recognize that first ewe in labor, so we were able to save the lamb and most of the others. I still think about Melissa bringing those two lambs back to life, and it takes my breath away.

Life took on a rhythm it hadn't before. I continued to do chores, and Melissa relaxed when she noticed the animals hadn't died under my two-days-a-week care. I still had enough energy left in my day to write, and to work. I was sort of a writer, I was sort of a farmer. I was no longer that woman in my dreams drowning, tangled in seaweed. I was a woman who felt most comfortable swimming with other writers, but when I needed to, I could crawl up onto shore, trade in my mermaid tail for a pair of legs and overalls, then do what needed to be done on the farm. Hey, that was it. A mermaid. A woman transformed. Half woman, half fish. Yes, this felt right. I was a Pisces, after all. Half writer, half farmer. Half city girl, half country girl. Half crazy, half sane.

I told my dad I was going to get a tattoo.

"Why?" he yelped.

"Because I think I've had a hell of a midlife crisis and I think I'm coming out of it. I want to mark the occasion with a tattoo."

Dad's face wrinkled. "I had a midlife crisis."

"I remember." He'd moped around the house for months the year he turned forty.

"But I didn't get a *tattoo,* for heaven's sake. I got a motorcycle."

"I remember."

My dad coughed. "Wouldn't you rather get a motorcycle?"

Ha. I told my mom and she immediately began worrying about infections from dirty needles. I assured her the tattoo artist was clean and conscientious. Mary had gone to her a few months before and the woman had tattooed a beautiful goat on Mary's shoulder—Miss May, the matriarch of her herd.

Spirit, the tattoo artist, sketched exactly what I had in mind. She photocopied the drawing onto a sheet of mimeograph paper, the smell transporting me instantly back to grade school, then placed that sheet on my body, rubbing it to transfer the design onto my skin. Melissa hovered nearby, watching out for dirty needles.

The tattooing took three hours, and the air conditioning in the building had failed, so we were all hot and sweaty. At the painful parts, I gripped my hands together, but said nothing. We sort-of-farmers are too tough to moan about a little thing like a razor-sharp needle piercing our tender skin repeatedly. Maybe I had some of my tough grandmother's genes after all.

Once the tattoo healed, I was so proud of the thing that I showed it to everyone who would stand still. Finally Melissa, who rarely criticized me, gently pointed out that perhaps I'd better stop lifting my shirt to every stranger I met.

Okay, okay, but the tattoo, for me, signaled the end of the most difficult transition of my life. I'd done it. I'd stuck it out, both the relationship and the farm. As I looked back over the last four years, I could see that while lots of things went wrong, more things went right. The things that went right just weren't funny enough or traumatic enough to remember.

My tattoo signaled a major shift in our lives. Our irritating and stressful ménage à trois was now a quartet: me, Melissa, the farm, and my writing. Four elements all needing balance and boundaries.

My family had been right about me, and wrong. I'm not farmer material, but I can be if Melissa needs me. I wear a six-inch tattoo of a mermaid on my back to prove it.

epilogue:
still crazy after all these years

it's been ten years since we started the farm, and I can hardly believe I'm the same person. When lambing rolls around every May, I now deliver lambs myself, tie off umbilical cords, and deliver shots. I can lance an abscess on a goat's jaw, pick fly maggots off a ewe's rump, and drive the tractor almost better than Melissa. . . .

Is anyone buying this? I certainly hope not. As we age, our basic personality traits intensify, so I still get anxious during lambing, do my best to avoid getting my hands dirty, and if given a choice between reading a book in the sun or putting in a few hours' of hard physical labor, we all know which I'd pick.

On the other hand, chores give me structure, they give me responsibility, they get me outside on days I'd usually never leave the house. I'm stronger than I've ever been. The other day I insisted my mother feel my bicep, feeling silly to be acting like a proud ten-year-old boy, but her wide eyes were gratifying. Yes, there is a muscle under all that cushion.

I pinch and cut fingers, bruise arms and legs, strain muscles, fall down, twist ankles, but most people do all that playing a vigorous game of tennis. I can use a pitchfork, machete, sledgehammer, mower, weed whacker, saw, hammer, wrench, bolt cutter, post pounder. Although I carry my own pocketknife now, Melissa still offers hers gallantly when needed. I chase sheep, wrestle with implements, drag heavy wooden pallets, and carry fifty-pound bags of corn.

Unfortunately, I've yet to spin wool into yarn, dye it, and knit our sweaters and socks in my vast spare time. I did purchase a spinning wheel, but it doesn't seem capable of doing much on its own, other than collecting dust.

Our sheep numbers fluctuate as the ewes from that original batch of ewe lambs are now getting quite old, and must be sold. But we keep young females to replace them. We continue to sell more meat through word of mouth, thanks to satisfied customers. We still don't name our sheep, but as one friend maintains, when Melissa calls out, "Good morning, 75," or, "Hi, 66," those numbers sound an awful lot like names.

Lance and Merlin, the two neutered goats, now live nearby on another farm, where they get more attention. Our barn cat, Oliver, adopted an orange kitten we cleverly named Pumpkin. Our llamas, Chachi and Zipper, continue to do their job; we know this because during the last lambing season a coyote stood on the other side of the fence early one morning, facing Melissa down. That he did not kill any lambs is testament to the value of guard llamas.

Our vineyard produces more each year, and we've done an excellent job of consuming the wine the winery makes from our grapes. We've finally gotten the weeds under control using an effective method. As I whisper to a select few friends who won't judge us, "Roundup is our friend."

One Valentine's Day Melissa gave me a touching present that brought instant tears of happiness to my eyes. Inside my card she'd tucked a check written to us for twenty-five dollars. Because she knew I hated them and their manure, Melissa the Poultry Lover sold those blasted "vineyard" geese to a crazy friend of ours. Now, that's love.

Melissa still has headaches, but after she took a friend's advice to eliminate chocolate and caffeine from her diet, the headaches decreased to the point she only has two or three a week, instead of seven.

I still think about those animals we've loved and lost: Moche the llama, Ambrosia the goat, our dogs Sasha, Tory, and Amber. Our current rooster is Tony, but we see in him shades of Serge, Sonny, El Guapo, and the others who came before him. A few years ago Mama Duck disappeared, likely taken by a bald eagle, the only bird strong enough to take on such a large duck. We've found a replacement who's doing great, but Melissa still talks about the original Mama Duck.

We continue to use goats as a milk source for bottle lambs, but because none of them will adopt lambs as Ambrosia did, we must milk the goats, then feed the lambs in bottles. Despite all that happens in the world, goats need to be milked, no matter how a farmer might feel. One morning as I sat in the barn, exhausted from life's stresses, leaning against the warm goat listening to her chew her cud while chickens scolded each other, milking a goat became a deeply moving experience. Farmers mourn or get stressed or have aches and pains like anyone else, but we must stay on our feet, doing what needs to be done.

Our two peacocks (long story, don't ask), brought an element of exotic elegance to the farm, until they began pooping on the hood of my car. All winter long they'd leave these grayish swirls of poop the size of a Dairy Queen ice cream cone, which froze solid to the hood. Of course, after I started the car and drove on the highway for a few minutes, the heat of the engine would thaw the poop, and it'd come flying toward my windshield at 65 miles per hour. The peacocks have, not surprisingly, left the farm.

Melissa wants cattle so badly she has already put it on this year's

Christmas list: one Jersey cow and calf. She won't be getting them, but it's only a matter of time before bovines join the ovines on this farm. Melissa and I continue to delight in each other's company, sense of humor, and support. I'm more willing to compromise, and so is she. Our underwear has now comingled in the same drawer for over twenty years.

I still do not have a doorknob on my office door. The other day our latest dog, Sophie, a half Great Dane, watched as Melissa once again bent over and peered at me through the hole in my door. The next day, when I heard heavy breathing, I looked up to find the Great Dane peering in at me. Can't a writer get *any* privacy around here?

I don't regret the farm. The animals enrich my life. How many people on a daily basis see newborn lambs cavorting in their back yard, llamas yawning with excitement as you bring their feed, or have a baby goat fall asleep in your lap? Some days, of course, I wish we owned nothing more than a goldfish so we were free to travel, but then that dream would obliterate Melissa's.

I still think boundaries are a good idea, but I've learned they need to breathe a little, just as a barn must breathe, and a relationship must breathe. Embracing the daily chaos of my life is a bit like trying to hug an octopus, but when I consider the alternatives—death or boredom—the chaos on a farm, on *our* farm, is beautiful.

I write nearly every day, and have sold three more children's books, all, ironically enough, inspired by the farm. I've written three novels for adults, as yet unpublished, but then, that's no longer why I write. Before we started the farm, I wrote only to publish, but now I know why those students in Marion's class all those years ago said they'd write even if they'd never be published. Publishing isn't enough of a reward to keep pushing yourself, to keep writing. You do it because you love it, because you can't stop. Turns out the same is true of farming.

acknowledgments

Writers need the support and encouragement of other
writers, and I've been surrounded by the best: Cindy
Rogers, Phyllis Root, Jane Resh Thomas, Janet Lawson, John Coy,
Jody Peterson Lodge, Selby Beeler, Heidi Magnuson, Laurel
Winter, Coleen Johnston, Alice Duggan, Barb Santucci, Mary
Casanova, Marsha Chall, Ann Monson, Kitty Baker, Maryann
Weidt, Lois Berg, and Kathleen Connelly. Without them this
book would have remained a series of little "pieces" I was too
timid to call "memoir."

Paulette Bates Alden and Marc Niesen pointed me in the right
direction—it was good that someone saw where I should go, since
I often couldn't.

I'm deeply grateful that my dedicated agent, Elizabeth Pomada,
found me just the right editor. This wise and witty editor, Renée
Sedliar, shepherded my book through Marlowe & Company
with such skill, grace, and contagious enthusiasm that I'm reluctant to share her with other authors.

Many thanks to all the farmers, shepherds, grape growers, and
sustainable farming folks who have taught me so much over the
years. My family—immediate and extended—are actually way

more supportive than any undergarment, and I'm grateful to have been raised by caring parents who did their best to teach me boundaries. My sister Sandy and her husband Rick are pretty cool, and I'm grateful she no longer bites me. Thanks to Melissa's mom, who cheered us on and dispensed advice as we started the farm.

And finally, the largest thanks (if thanks can have a size) goes to Melissa. While it is true she dragged me into farming, a path I never would have chosen on my own, I really don't mind. It has been, and continues to be, quite a ride.